Style*

POWER

POWER

UNLOCK THE CONNECTION BETWEEN YOUR SOUL AND YOUR
WARDROBE… AND SET YOURSELF FREE IN STYLE

ISBN: 978-0-6451605-0-5
E-book ISBN: 978-0-6451605-1-2

Book cover photography: Hipster Mum Photography
Book cover design: Mae Branding
Book layout: JuJu Creative Hub
Printed on demand and distributed by IngramSpark

To my three wise men, your love, light and laughter
are my fuel to shine brighter every day.

Contents

PILLAR THREE: (UN)CONVENTIONAL STYLE TOOLS

IMPLEMENTING THE STYLE POWER FORMULA

When you look at clothes and the energy you put into them as an opportunity for your essence to shine through, magic happens.

~ ALMA BARRERO

STYLE POWER

Bienvenid@

Welcome to a new era, a new dimension, a new expression of who you truly are.

This is a space to allow your inner child, your soul and your sacred body to create as one.

I invite you to open your mind and get ready to reimagine what style is or at least what it means to you.

You're here to open the doors to a new life. And yes, we're still talking about clothes, but on a deeper level, a level that will impact the way you go about everything, a level that will lift your spirit, your confidence and the way you show up every single day.

It will create an impact on the way your message, your words and your mission land for others.

But most importantly, it will give you a new way of looking at life with love, honour and celebration of yourself in a way you have never looked before.

Whether you're a female, male, transgender, non-gender, human, or extra-terrestrial being, this book doesn't go there. We all have a body, we all have a soul, and we all know what harmony, exaltation and personal power are. That's all you need to make use of this book in reaching a new level on your journey of self-discovery and connection to your divine essence.

My ultimate goal is to expand myself, helping you to expand yourself, to set myself free, setting you free also. And then, we will see how that ripple effect means that your light, in turn, will positively impact others in the world.

I'm ready and you know you're ready too. I ask only one more thing before we get started: *trust and relax.*

This will not be a right-or-wrong type of journey. It'll be the perfectly imperfect highway to your ultimate self-expression and outburst of unique light.

I love you. Let's do this!

Alma x

Are you up for a soulful makeover? *

WALKING TOGETHER TOWARDS THE LIGHT... IN STYLE

I love you. And this book is the ultimate reflection of this energy. I want to thank you for being here. It's my absolute honour to allow this message to come through me. Having you here to receive it means the world to me.

I believe I'm in this world for the "simple" purpose of guiding humans to their inner light.

I believe I'm here to ignite that vibrant, magnificent light inside of you.

Because the truth is, even if it means nothing to you – and you wouldn't be reading this if it meant nothing to you – your light is vital both for you and for the world.

I believe that incandescent light you have inside is what makes us all better, but most importantly, it's what makes *you* feel like you're stepping right into the middle of your power sphere. Right in the middle.

Personal power is something everybody needs to have at its maximum level if we want this journey called life to be a lifetime without regrets.

Not that I believe that we *should* regret anything by the end, but I believe we'll all leave this earth from a much more peaceful, trusting and surrendered space if we're able to do this magic walk, stepping confidently in the most truthful way.

And this trusting and truthful existence comes from showing up aligned with the most brilliant and powerful aspects of yourself.

In 2000, I saw a movie that changed my expectations in life. The movie was *The Kid*. In it, Bruce Willis is an image consultant and a good one. He had an innate gift of seeing the potential and hidden truth in each person.

This really struck me! I was like the cat in one of those cat videos pouncing on the dots of light. Seeing this movie was no accident. I believe every single thing that happens in our life happens *for* us, not *to* us.

At the time, I was 17 and completely unaware of what 'purpose' was. I had no clue what it meant to follow divine guidance. All I knew about God was what I'd been told in my Catholic upbringing, and I was in that rebellious phase where the only reason I went to church was because it was kind of enforced.

That day, watching Bruce Willis, I saw the light. Even though I was young and unaware, I still saw it. And I've been following that dot of light for as long as I can remember.

Here's the problem. When we get caught up in all of life's distractions, that takes us away from our light. But I *know* you can live from that power sphere. I *know* you can shine unapologetically and radiantly from within. I *know* you're here to show up more than you ever have before.

With this book, I invite you to hop on my elegant, passionate, powerful horse and let me lead you all the way to paradise, where this animal will become a beautiful brown Pegasus and where you'll give yourself permission to enter a life of freedom connected to your highest self.

From that space, you will create amazing outfits in seconds. From that space, you have the freedom to be your authentic self and shine from within.

I am writing this book to guide, expand and set millions of people free of self-judgement, trying to fit in, expectations, and external limitations that don't belong to them and never did or never will. I'm here to change the paradigm, to shed new light on the relationship we have with ourselves and to celebrate connecting with our inner guidance, with every single cell of our sacred body. I'm here to help us learn to listen to that inner wisdom and honour this sacred space with clothes, accessories, makeup or whatever we're called to use as a joyful vehicle to set *free* our wildest and purest self.

I bring the brown Pegasus, and you bring your personal symbol of freedom, a symbol that will allow you to sit nice and cosy, close to that essence of yours. You won't need to share your symbol with anybody else. Nobody else needs to understand your language, your self-love, your journey. It's something that concerns only you.

Similarly, nobody needs to understand that I see my mission as divine, spiritual and deep, even though they may see clothes as a lavish, superficial commodity. I'm not into fashion runways or style rules, but I am here to open the door of possibility and self-empowerment to *you* in a new way. I'm here to write about self-expansion. Clothes are simply the fun, entertaining way that my inner child expresses some of that.

Once you achieve certain levels of awareness, the clothes themselves won't matter. In fact, you may feel a healthy detachment and see healthy potential in getting to know more about clothing at the same time. You will notice how your body breathes in certain colours or fabrics, and there'll be no going back.

As your filter changes, your perception heightens, your sensitivity to dressing in a soul-fuelling way increases, and your inner child and sacred body blend in a magical way, you will see how you were always meant to feel **100% you** in your clothes. You'll stop comparing yourself with others when it comes to style because you'll understand you have nobody to compare yourself with. Your light is *yours* to dress. Nobody else gets to experience your light the way you do.

You'll mind your own business and mind your own style for that matter too! Imagine a world where everybody saw clothing as an opportunity to pay tribute to themselves and to remind themselves constantly how much love we have towards ourselves when we stand in our essence.

Imagine a world where we let others know it's possible to live *that* connected, giving them permission to shine their own light.

Imagine a world where we allow others to feel so reassured that they give even more people permission to shine *their* own light too.

Imagine a world where you feel so certain that when others react – and they will – you'll still be okay.

Because when you find yourself in the middle of your power sphere, having built a foundation of self-love and a mountain of **inner-outer connection,** nobody can make that crumble. Nobody can change or disrupt your perfectly imperfect connection to yourself.

And that's freaking magnificent.

I'm here to give you the language, the permission and the space to organise that sacred celebration of yourself so that you can enjoy the ripple effect of empowering others in turn.

SO, WHAT ARE YOU SIGNING UP FOR?

This journey is like doing a style course blended with spirituality and a whole lot of joy. It will be divine channelling work mixed with clothes.

There'll be moments where you might resist the information because it won't make sense from a 3D reality perspective. I want to honour that you may have those thoughts, and that's okay because they're valid. You're here to open a new door, not walk the path you've already walked.

When I speak of God, the Universe, the Divine or the Force, it might be confronting for you. For the same reason, because of your convictions, whether religious or non-religious beliefs, you might resist following some of what this book says.

Instead of resisting, you can simply substitute that word to whatever you want to call that gut sensation you've surely had in the past, that hunch of something inexplicable calling you, that feeling of being attracted to something or someone. If you're a parent, call that the moment your two-year-old was about to fall and you grabbed her in the last millisecond before her head hit the pavement. If you aren't, call that the moment you decided to call or message a friend and they call or message you as you reach for your phone or that random song you were singing that suddenly plays on the radio.

We can call it magic too.

If you're open to the idea that there's a higher force here supporting you, and if you're willing to let that force help you to trust, and if you let that force's divine wisdom pour into everything you do… magic happens.

That's how I believe this book was created.

So, if style, spirituality, self-discovery and self-advancement are the words that characterise this work, you may ask…

WHY IS SPIRITUALITY EMBEDDED IN A STYLE BOOK?

Everyone who knows me and my work will be familiar with how hard I've fought to have a deeper style message than the typical one you see every day in the mainstream. Many people will disregard it, and that's okay because we're not taught to be authentically ourselves.

It took me a long time to refine my style process because the concepts of trusting the Universe, living different lifetimes and doing energetic work don't exactly blend well with the religious principles I grew up with as a member of a conservative, Catholic family.

When I was in university, I experienced a big disconnection with my faith because I didn't understand certain messages I learned in church that I interpreted as discriminatory. This was my interpretation, but to mention a few, I struggled with messages like: those who are divorced couldn't be eligible to take communion; same-sex marriages aren't to be consecrated in church; homosexuality was not considered a natural tendency; people should feel shame and guilt for having certain thoughts and behaviours.

I didn't understand the concept of God *punishing* us for doing *bad* things. In my gut, the whole idea of punishment didn't blend with the perception of an omnipresent higher power.

Now, these are *very* simplistic interpretations, but this was how my kid brain conceived religion.

Fast forward to 27 and discovering the magic of self-development and spirituality. I started finding all the beauty and uplifting aspects of soooo many messages I received as a kid within the religion I was taught. Messages like: God is in every one of us; Christ saw God in all humans, no matter what they did.

I learned that we don't get punished, but it's all part of a synchronised creation. In other words, it's all energy. There's the law of reciprocity, the law of attraction, the benefits of following your true path and taking inspired action. There's "ask and it's given", which works in so many ways.

When I stayed out of the *dogma* and allowed myself to dig deeper into spiritual synchronicities between Catholicism and other religions, the doors to my own spirituality opened wide. So wide, in fact, that I felt a profound transformation, in a sense becoming part of the *whole*.

I felt **more connected than ever** to those who practised spirituality, no matter how it looked. I felt more connected to everyone. Somehow, it all made sense, and I never looked back.

I experience this connection through the knowledge that there's a highest self inside all of us, and the nature of that self is God. That's how we are all part of the whole. That's how magic happens in *everything* and *everyone*.

And style was an important part of this too.

I wrote this book in 2020 when the Covid-19 pandemic was exploding. All the business investments and choices I made during that time were a reflection of how much I trusted the process and my divine inner wisdom. And how peaceful and joyful it is to live from this state!

Do I have moments of doubt and fear? You bet! Do I let them win? No, because I have a support team who are there to keep me on track and remind me I'm not falling for that crap anymore.

I decided to pick a lane. And in that lane, only magic is allowed.

Some days, it's a fast getaway from "worry town". Other days, it takes a bit more persistence.

But once my awareness reaches a new level, it's uncomfortable to stay in those old states of self-doubt, feeling like a failure or needing to be perfect. Maybe you notice the same thing. Perhaps you feel like who you are now could never fit back inside who you used to be. It's called spiritual growth!

In my style career, I didn't mention my spiritual growth within my style message. The real reason? I didn't want to turn off anybody who doesn't believe in a higher power. But then this book came to me, and I couldn't hold it back. I felt the pouring forth of information every day. This is a crucial part of who I am and what I stand for.

If, by sharing this spiritual style process I can help just one other person dig deeper into that inner connection to get a real transformation, then my work has fulfilled its purpose. Maybe that person is you.

We do nobody any favours when we show up as someone we're not. The reason why commoditised style messages don't sit well with me is because, as you'll see in this book, I want to give you the opportunity to dig much deeper into yourself than mainstream style advice allows.

I believe there's an opportunity to grow through the exploration of your spiritual self and your style in the most incredible ways. And I hope by the end of this book you'll have seen what I mean by that.

WELCOME TO PARADISE

The day I saw my purpose clearly I was on the road leading you to paradise. I pictured the road to Hana in Maui with a paradise at the end. Together, we get there on my brown horse that transforms itself by growing wings. Notice it doesn't transform into a multi-coloured, crazy-sparkly white unicorn. Nope, my Pegasus just grows wings because this is my symbol of freedom. It's your permission to enter a paradise (AKA life after this book) and set yourself free.

Free of self-judgement.
Free of expectations.
Free of self-limitations.

We might blame others for our limitations, but here is the truth: nobody entered your head and created a limitation for you. You gave your consent, whether consciously or subconsciously. Your highest self chose everything in your life. To paraphrase Eleanor Roosevelt, nobody can make you feel anything without your permission.

So, as we enter this paradise, leave our friend victimhood at the door. There's only one way to true transformation, and it's taking responsibility and owning all the good and all the not so good, all the gifts and all the circumstances, the good feelings and the bad.

Our dear friends Shame and Guilt are also lovingly parked next to the bamboo revolving door at the entrance. Here, in paradise, you're free. You can create the vision of yourself in the mirror without letting in old stories of age, parenthood, external expectations, family rules, body shape or self-limiting beliefs get in the way.

Welcome to *possibility*.

WHY ME?

This is the question that I ask the Universe about my mission of helping you get closer to who you are and dressing for it. The same image keeps popping into my head: it's one where all of my clients unveil more of themselves. It's like a weight is lifted and they see themselves in the mirror again.

At one point in our life, we were connected to who we are. It was a time when the external doctrines, dogmas and ways of life wouldn't actually sink in, at least not enough to interfere with our sense of knowing.

I was a happy and beautiful six-year-old girl who loooooved being quirky, dancing and gymnastics. I didn't care what others said; I just loved doing my thing. As well as doing my dolls' hair. Oh yes, that was my thing too. In fact, when I was a teenager, I wanted to be a hairdresser, but I was told that, while hairdressing was lovely, first I needed to go to uni. It's funny to think of that now we have so much freedom of choice.

The true reason I ended up doing a bachelor in business in uni was that I was already out of touch by this time that I had no idea what else to do. The options in my hometown weren't numerous, and any other career I suggested at home was either: too hard to qualify in, too difficult to find a job afterwards or a non-uni option (which wasn't an option).

Although I knew deep inside by that time that I wanted to become an image consultant, it was ridiculous to suggest it. For starters, there was no such career in Spain that people knew, apart from image advisors to politicians. That was pretty much all I was able to identify in the outside world. I still remember the days in my corporate job as a financial auditor when I'd just speak my mind and say what I really wanted to do, and my colleagues would look at me thinking, *this woman is nuts…*

How is a financial auditor going to have a career that is so little-known, let alone be in-demand by clients.

Eventually, an official training in image consulting was created in Spain but the program wasn't what I was looking for. I was more interested in the internal shift experienced when aligning the outside façade with the person, but at that point in my life, I only knew I wanted to help people look their best.

I met with a couple of image consultants who existed at the time, and I just wasn't attracted to the model of business. One was a colour trainer, and that was pretty much all she did. The other, who I thought was going to be my mentor, soon changed her business to running an aesthetician clinic; again, not what I wanted.

The time came when I started dating my fun, caring, awesome now-husband Tomás. Within a year of dating (having been friends before), we knew that we wanted to see the world and learn English. (In theory, improve our English, but what we learned in school didn't get us close to the level we needed!)

One thing led to another and we ended up in Canada where I found my first image consulting mentor and took the training that had been awaiting me for so long. It was exactly what I wanted. I began exploring image consulting as a holistic practice and how people's energy could be positively affected by my work. And that training shifted my life in every aspect.

Fast forward another 10 years, and I keep reinventing my business as I grow. I started with a one-on-one in-person business and now run my style consultancy fully online, talking at events and doing my best to inspire people to show up with their best idea of self in mind and in their clothes.

That is how I got here and where I plan to take you through this book. Shall we get started?

The Style Power Formula*

The purpose of this book is to help you achieve deep transformation and create that connection between your soul and your wardrobe in the most effortless of ways, honouring yourself through your expression.

My Style Power Formula™ is the result of more than 10 years' experience, including highs and lows, celebrations and mistakes, working with people from all over the world. Understand that this is the one and only formula that works if you want the reflection in the mirror to be a reflection of who you truly are – effortlessly.

This formula has three pillars:

1. **Sense of Self:** learning how to connect with your true light.
2. **Roadmap to Style Empowerment**: creating an empowered style vision and identity.
3. **(Un)conventional Style Tools:** using Colour Magic, Personality Styles and Visual Game, a twist on conventional style advice.

What you will obtain as a result of applying these three pillars into your life is: being **100% you** from the inside out!

In other words:

Sense of Self + Empowered Vision and Identity +
(Un)conventional Style Tools

=

100% you from the inside out

As you'll see, external style tools only make up one of the three pillars, so one third of the total formula. I don't see any point in clothes that don't take self-expression and future vision into account. Like, none.

Put it this way. Is it the same feeling when you eat ice cream as when I *tell* you about eating ice cream? Do you enjoy ice cream as much when I *tell* you the flavour and type that you need to get or if *you* choose the ice cream for yourself by checking in with what you want? You feel best when you choose the ice cream you feel like eating, right?

It's the same with clothes.

It's one thing to have a special red carpet event and hire event stylists, hair and makeup professionals to create a perfect look; they know about specific lighting, atmosphere, etc. But it's another thing to get ready in the morning for your everyday life.

Having control and ownership of how you want to feel when wearing clothes will get you more and more excited about how you show up. The Style Power Formula shows you just how much power you can feel within yourself and express on the outside.

Over the course of this book, we will explore these three pillars, so that you can achieve that connection with your inner self, create a vision of who you are and understand how to show it. As we go through, I've also included special Style Power Practices for you to integrate what you're learning and take concrete steps towards your own empowerment in style. Use them as a guide for exploring this work, but don't get hung up on doing them 'perfectly' or completely. As you'll soon discover, that's not my style!

Wherever you are on this journey, you're ready. Because it's never too late or too early to start discovering your true self.

PILLAR ONE

Sense of Self

OWN YOUR POWER AND DRESS FOR IT.

Creating that uplifting and life-changing connection
with your wardrobe will start with your inner work. In
this first part of the Style Power Formula, I'm going to
help you get in touch with that magnificent light of yours
as well as with your body's wisdom. You'll understand
how important this first pillar is for achieving that
unexplainable energetically perceived sense of self, that
magnetism. And that will translate into effortless style and
dressing intuitively every morning.

STYLE POWER

CHAPTER ONE

Connect with your true light *

YOUR LIGHT

I see your light as that divine inner force that contains all the ingredients that make you uniquely who you are – without filters. Your light is confident, ambitious, unlimited, abundant. Your light lets you live from possibility, not from circumstance.

When we're able to tap into our light, we can listen to what our body has to say, what those voices that belong to us say and how they dissipate.

Your light is so incredibly powerful that there's no other being that can dim it. Even going through years of taming and being told to be "good", your light is still there, waiting for you to realise the reality that you can achieve whatever you want. You're already all those attributes you want to be: bold, elegant, graceful, handsome, fabulous, stylish, wise, beautiful, powerful, a one-of-a-kind, smart, strong, whatever they are for you.

If you think about it, by dimming your light, there's one less thing to "worry" about for those who want to keep you 'under control'. And I'm not talking about anyone specific here, but also I'm talking about a lot of people! From some individuals' opinions to religious organisations' beliefs, to governments' actions, to family dogmas, to company cultures…

But that's not how your light wants to come through. Your light doesn't compare itself to anybody. There's no competence at being you. There's no *other* when it comes to being more or less. There's only one purpose: to shine brighter so that you contribute to the highest good of all, to illuminate others with your grace and to inspire them with your light and to help them follow that path. (And if you want a religious analogy, imagine how the three wise men followed the star to Jesus in Bethlehem.)

What I'd love you to understand is that when you tap into that light and dress from that place, your message will be 100 times more powerful, your impact will be much more expansive, and this will only happen through trust and connection with your ultimate highest self. If you'd just let that light of yours shine...

Now, I'm not saying this is all fun and roses. When you start shining your light, those who haven't been able to tap into theirs can have two reactions: wanting to follow you and adore you or telling you, 'who do you think you are?' But here's the powerful part. When you're in that state of alignment with your light, there's no word or remark or look powerful enough to dim you.

We are human, and we do fall off our path, but the important factor here is: once you're able to tap into that light of yours and unblock the energy keeping you from it, there's no going back! You are the path! There's no falling off. There's only momentum.

Your new inspired way of dressing will be embedded within you. Even if one day you don't like what you see, it doesn't mean you've lost your mojo. Trust me on this. Writing this book reminds me, too, that even on days when I feel complete garbage, those who've seen my light always see me as *fabulous*. And that's why feeling the love and allowing that love to come through is so rejuvenating and the perfect medicine to go to sleep and wake up the next day with fresh, self-loving eyes.

So, what do you think 'light' means in all of this? Your light is your purest form of energy, your essence on steroids. Your light is when your power expands, and your brilliant genius is set free. We all have this unique light, and I'm here to tell you that you must keep digging deeper into it – always!

One day while I was in the course of writing this book, I saw a post on social media about the sheer number of people who had to come together since the beginning of humanity for you to be here in this moment. It spoke to me, which is why I'm sharing it now. How can we disregard such a simple yet incredible idea? You're here to complete a 'duty'. Whether you know what that is yet or not, working to acknowledge your unique essence will 100% keep you on track.

The Sense of Self pillar (and the rest of the *Style Power* book!) will help you refine your process of self-discovery. It is a constantly evolving sacred process. And when others perceive that harmony you exude, they'll want whatever you're having! They'll want a taste of that freedom, and it'll be up to you how (or if) you let them be part of your expansion.

You and I know you're meant for great things. As soon as you allow for that to develop, the sooner you'll start harvesting the fruits of your constant growing effort.

There's *no one* in this world with your light, and it is your responsibility to contribute that unique light to the world. This is why you're here. I love you, I love myself, and this expression of love is what led us here to our time together in this book.

HOW TO DRESS YOURSELF

Dressing ourselves is something we learnt when we were little. I find myself teaching my kids how to dress themselves now. But is there more to it than simply grabbing clothes that match, that fit and that are appropriate for what you're doing today? Well, yes.

Let me put it this way. Is there something else behind your skin? Is there any activity underneath that we can't see on the surface? Is the sky as we see it, or is there more out there? Is it truly blue, or is it an optical effect? There's always another magical layer to every magnificent thing, including you, so how could there not be deeper meaning when it comes to getting dressed?

I see style as an illusion when it comes to 3D reality. You can create any illusion you want with the right knowledge, and you're going to learn about that here. I also see style as a subconscious-conscious wand that can help you influence others in a powerful way. Most importantly, I see style as a means of influencing and connecting with that side of yourself that *you* want to expand, even if your brain tells you that's impossible...

Get this right now. If you see it, it's possible. If you appreciate it, it's somewhere inside of you. Otherwise, you wouldn't even notice it.

You just need to allow yourself to align with that possibility in all the ways you can and honour that desire with your clothes. That's the first handy step you can take today towards being truly you. By having something you want in your mind, it is already created.

So, the next question is:

How do you dress yourself?

Well, you would ask:

How do you want to feel today?

Then ask your wardrobe to show you some ways.

You want to feel unstoppable, maybe? You want to feel loving, nurturing? You want to feel sexy, attractive? Comfortable but stylish? Elegant and unique?

Then think of how you can feel this way in your day-to-day and just *go for it*! Respect your inner wisdom, and you'll find the life of your dreams. Ignore it, and you'll keep finding a wall blocking your way.

Believe in that deeper layer:

- When you cook happily rather than begrudgingly, your food will taste better when you eat it and feel differently in your body.
- If you bless your water and connect with it, it'll have a different effect on your body when you drink it.
- When you smile at others, even when you don't feel like it, it'll brighten their day and give a nice boost to your endorphins.

No matter what others say, you're here, a miracle, and deserve to dress however you feel, according to your nature.

I used to feel so out of touch with my style. Not knowing what to wear or how to wear it. Always admiring others' sense of style but never feeling happy with mine. Always seeing myself as too fat, too wide, too thick, too tall, too short… I'm getting to a place of acceptance, but you know the way

I got here? Time, age, the fact that I don't want my kids to see a mother who doesn't own her beauty, the message that I've been sharing for years and some highly effective tools I've adopted that have created new neural pathways in my brain, seeing the beauty, owning it and highlighting the journey; these are the things that have allowed me to be here today for you.

So, I've been there, and I get it. I know what it's like to beat yourself up on low days when you don't like what you see in the mirror. But I'm here to tell you it's all part of being human, and you can shift your attention. The key is awareness and your power to choose where you place your attention because wherever you choose to place your attention, it expands. Choose wisely.

YOU'RE BEYOND POWERFUL

I feel it now. I've always been much more powerful than I thought. And I believe you can also have some of this medicine.

When you realise your power is infinite and you're powerful beyond measure...

When you realise anything you set your mind to is possible and trust you'll get the how by *taking action*...

When you let that light of yours come through...

...magic happens!

Those who meet you will be open to negotiate with you, will be open to starting conversations, will be open to letting your light enlighten them.

When you let that light shine through, you'll stand in your power and it'll be much more difficult to allow anybody to tell you that you're anything other than what you wholeheartedly believe you are.

Are you ready to start healing and showing up for yourself, making the best style choices for you?

I promise to give you the most actionable and simple style advice you've ever come across.

The one thing that'll set this book apart is that everybody can use it. Because I don't follow external cookie-cutter patterns when it comes to clothing. I follow your light only.

PERCEPTION MATTERS

Do you ever look at pictures from the past and think, *huh, I looked good,* but maybe at the time that picture was taken you didn't feel that way at all?

Do you realise our brains are so powerful that they make us see things that actually aren't even real, especially when it comes to how we judge our appearance and/or behaviour?

I still look at pictures from a year ago and think, *I actually didn't look that bad.* In fact, I look great; that fat or cellulite I used to see isn't even there, or if it is, it looks beautiful to me. And yet, it's exhausting the amount of chatter my brain can contain when I look in the mirror – sometimes to the point that what I see I think is ugly.

These days, I choose to wake up in the morning and say to myself in the mirror that I love myself.

The goal of letting go of the exhausting chatter and loving ourselves is to be at peace with our pictures now. If you can't be at peace, then don't look at the pictures today, don't weigh yourself, don't trigger that inner mean version of yourself that's *so* not you. Wait until you're in a better mood.

Move your attention because you deserve better. Remember, your life is where you put your attention, so ask yourself how you want to *be*.

When you came to this world, you didn't arrive with all that self-judgement, did you? It's a matter of being patient and acknowledging what needs to be unlearned so that you can get closer to your true essence.

Our state of mind changes our perceptions. Our hunger, anxiety, tiredness alter our brain, lower our guard and change our perceptions. Your life is all perception, and you're responsible for adapting those perceptions to what you want your reality to be. Be aware that life isn't how it is, but how we see it, so ask yourself how you want to see.

When you feel out of touch with yourself and a failure because you're not able to make that sale, hit that deadline, or pick the kids up from school every day, remember that where you're at could seem excellent to someone else.

When you're trying to find that pair of high boots that fit your calves, and you can't find them, remember not to make it about your calves (yes, I've been there too), and instead realise there are different boots for different people.

It's not about you. It's about finding the right boot, or jacket, or dress that fits you perfectly.

We need to stop taking it out on our self-worth every time something doesn't look the way we want. We need to remove self-sabotage from our daily routine.

Of course, we all self-sabotage at some point or other, but those who are highly aware can change their thoughts immediately and raise the bar in order to not let their personal power be affected by what happens.

We need to realise that, just like we're all different, there are millions of brands and shapes and pieces for everyone. We can believe an ill-fitting boot means it's hard to find the right clothes or we can choose to think it's easy to find clothes. Try out this affirmation:

"Clothes come to me effortlessly at the perfect time in the perfect way."

Now apply this rule to e v e r y single thing you want to attract in your life, money included. Instead of creating your reality from a place of need, start creating it from a place of want. Instead of operating from a place of lack, go about your life from a place of abundance.

And why not let it be easy?

THE POWER OF RECEIVING AND LOVING YOURSELF

Awareness about receiving has changed my life so much that I now carry a receiving journal where I write down all I receive every day. The aspects you focus your energy on expand. From money to gifts, to acts of kindness, to a simple 'I love you', a hug or somebody opening the door for you, pay attention and see how life changes when you are open to receiving.

How can you tap into the power of receiving?

Well, first, repeat after me: "I love myself", now feel it, "I love myself", feel it harder, "I love myself", embrace all it means, "I deeply love myself".

Open your eyes wide and hug that love in.

Secondly, when you start receiving compliments as you implement these tools, receive them always. Never disregard a compliment. Own it and believe it. You've earned that compliment, so wear that badge proudly and unapologetically because if you're going to feel sad about bad feedback or critique, you damn sure have to celebrate those compliments twice as hard to compensate!

Will you do that for me?

If you find it hard to say "I love myself", there's a book called *Love Yourself Like Your Life Depends On It* that help you to make this practice a habit.

And remember, love is what makes you whole. Let that shine of yours come through and allow yourself to look amazingly, stunningly, irresistibly you. Because you're divine, and that's your true nature.

From now on, pay attention to what role love plays in your relationship with yourself and others and not just your family. How much love are you allowing? Notice how much true love you ignore, yet how much attention and energy you waste on any sign that's the opposite of love.

It's time to receive and own your full power. And dress for it, won't you?

. . . .

Tools to upgrade your inner connection

Ask, and it is given; trust, and it's already coming; move, and you'll see the next step. This is how you gain momentum, but it starts with sitting, accepting, allowing and being with yourself. And take it from an overthinker, these tools can be game-changers!

1. Meditation

Practising meditation and choosing an outfit might seem like water and oil, but if you've made it this far, you'll understand that this book isn't about clothes but about establishing that connection with yourself so that you can make confident, empowered choices.

Meditation is a practice that can help you do that, but it took me a while to get. All the successful people would talk about it, but whenever I tried to pick it up, my brain would be so busy that I'd just stop after five minutes max.

Fast forward to today, I crave my meditation, and my kids believe I do it to live. And that's kind of true.

How did I get to this point where I need meditation like I need air and water? I started using some tricks to keep my brain entertained. Once I was able to find peace and joy from stillness, meditation became something that I needed to do rather than something I "had to" do.

The biggest shift that got me hooked on this practice was trusting myself and letting go of perfection. For example:

- Taking the time to listen to my body and how it wants to meditate that day.
- Choosing a spot that makes me feel at peace and asking my body what kind of music I need.
- Playing binaural beats, soothing sounds for your brain. (There are millions of different sounds you can try; the key is finding the one your body enjoys at the time.)
- Focusing on receiving first, allowing my energy to open

and then setting the intention and asking my guides help on whatever I'm currently focusing on.
- Pulling a card from a deck and concentrating on it whenever my mind would wander.
- Having a mantra to go back to when I notice myself thinking.

And because I believe in the power of mantras, here are some that came to me. Why not try some of them for yourself, paying attention to your body? If there's one that resonates, use it in your meditation and repeat it as many times during the day as you can:

"I allow myself to feel powerful, magnetic, attractive and creative."

"I give thanks for my permanent self-love and inspiration pouring through me."

"Thank you for the constant connection with my highest-self and with my body, bring me more please."

"I allow myself to see me past my clothes, my body and my expectations."

"I allow myself to feel worthy of receiving this magic wisdom that comes from within and dressing in a way that lights me up."

"I allow myself to shine because that's how I help myself and others to shine their light."

"I allow the masters and the divine within me to express itself through the way I dress myself every day, through the way I expand in my career, life and conversations."

"I trust the divine change and allow greatness in all its forms coming into my life."

"Universe, show me the way."

There's no right or wrong in this practice. Once we get over that place of judgement, it becomes all about en*joy*ment of feeling inside your body and allowing it to be easy.

On days when my mind is more cluttered, I've found journaling to be profoundly healing, which brings me to the next tool.

2. Soul journaling

One of my coaches and mentors, Patty Dominguez, brought this magic habit into my life. In fact, this practice gave birth to this book.

Here's how it works. Set the timer for a few minutes and play binaural beats or other music that helps you get into a magical, meditative state. Then allow the writing to flow. No thinking. Just allow the messages to come through. Try not to use this time to complain or write *egoic* thoughts. Simply allow inspiring thoughts to come through.

The amount of downloads I've had with this exercise has been amazing.

3. Walking meditations

Some days, sitting down and focusing on your breath isn't what you need, so walking meditations are a great way to connect with your essence and find that inspiration.

Even if it's a 20-minute walk for your mental health, get moving and connect with your body. You need those endorphins if you're going to reconnect with yourself. And I know you can do it.

Try playing meditative music or walking in complete silence. Alternatively, walk with headphones listening to audio books or podcasts that help you create more space to grow. (These are my medicine after intense days at home. I come back home like new every day I do it.)

Walking has been part of my self-care routine when I couldn't do more intense exercise, for example, when I was struggling to maintain my energy levels. I used to think, *Why would I go walking? It's just not exercise!* I used to be a full-on, heart-rate-to-the-max-or-nothing kind of woman. Maybe you can understand why I got into adrenal fatigue! Little did I know those walks I took when recovering from my illness would be just as healing as sleep and eating the right foods.

I realised it's the subtle movement and the stillness in nature that inspires the Divine to come through.

4. Self-hypnosis

I discovered the unlimited power of hypnosis through one of my mentors, Jim Fortin.

I'd had a hypnosis session in the past, and it had been powerful, but practising self-hypnosis daily changed my life.

When you think of hypnosis, you may worry that you'll pass out or not remember anything, but it's actually a completely different experience from what you may expect.

I look at self-hypnosis as a visualisation, quiet time to train your subconscious mind into being whatever you seek to be. Be it at peace, empowered, confident, focused or brave, you can condition your mind to be any identity you see yourself as in your ideal picture. This practice will help you make the most of this book, especially later on when we talk about style identities.

There are thousands of resources online to train yourself in self-hypnosis, from weight loss to quitting smoking to finding inner peace.

I can't even tell you how much this daily practice has changed my life and allowed me to achieve my goals, being already in my mind the person who achieves them.

5. Dreaming

Your soul dreams those dreams; not your body, not your mind. Those dreams come true. The soul travels all over the world when you dream.
~ CHIPPEWA ELDER JOHN THUNDERBIRD

In many cultures, dreams are far more important than most of us raised in modern western culture were taught to believe. In certain Native American cultures, it's said that we actually live when we're sleeping and sleep when we're awake. There's plenty of history around Dreamtime in Australian Aboriginal cultures and other sources of ancient wisdom.

I like to think of sleep as a time for soul magic when our body is in a complete state of relaxation, and our ego doesn't interfere.

One of my everyday tools to tap into divine wisdom is my dreams:

Before going to sleep, I ask my subconscious about anything I need to know in life or business. Most times, I receive the answer.

It's also important to ask to remember the next day. It's handy to have a notebook next to your bed so you don't forget like I do. If you do forget, your dream might still come back to you as a sign during the day, or you might recall having dreamt something a few days later.

The most magical, aligned people in my life run their life in dream time. I'm learning to master this practice, as I only started recently, and it takes some time of unlearning to master it, but I highly recommend you ask your dream double self or your subconscious mind a question that you need answered, and wait for a dream, song or sign to bring you the answer.

To give you an idea of how much this tool has helped me know myself more, there was a time I kept dreaming that I would never finish my exams. (It was a real nightmare!) I haven't had that dream in a while. Another time, I would dream that I was still dating ex-boyfriends. (At the time of writing, I've been with my beloved twin flame husband for more than 12 years.) I've also dreamed of people who have made me feel less in my life. (Of course, nobody can make you feel anything without your permission.)

All those dreams had one thing in common: situations in the past when I was where I didn't want to be, but because of life, family traditions, fears of being alone, constantly ignoring the voice of light within myself when it urged me to stay away from certain hurt souls or from lovely boyfriends that made me feel safe…

I kept pushing because that's what brave, obedient, nice people do, right? R i g h t ? Wrong!

That's what we're taught when we're very little – to keep our head down and be no trouble.

But we have all the answers within ourselves, and our dreams are just one proof of that, one more tool we can use to support our growth. Why don't you start experimenting with dreams as a way of discovering that inner connection?

6. Move

Kinesiology sessions, energy healing, lots of silence, cooking, playing with my kids, walking by the beach, walking with my family, dancing like nobody is watching… the list goes on. All these activities give you the opportunity to connect with your body and tap into that space where you're connected to yourself and have breakthroughs.

I highly recommend you go for it and start experimenting with all the tools that I share here, but before you do, stop and sit with yourself in stillness. If meditating feels far reach, play some binaural beats and let yourself write your thoughts.

Style Power Practice:
SOUL JOURNALING FOR SELF-KNOWLEDGE

Get comfortable with your journal and sit in stillness. Before you start, remind yourself that nobody will read what you write, so give yourself the luxury of time in your own company.

Now, soul journal on these prompts:

1. Write down all that comes to mind about who you are.
2. Write about what sets your heart on fire when you are without fear.

After connecting with yourself more deeply, you'll be able to start following the style tools in the remainder of this book, expanding your intuition and shining from within.

I love you. You're safe. You're well taken care of. And you can believe in the magic of your truthful light.

STYLE POWER

CHAPTER TWO

Inner-outer harmony *

LIVING A TRUE LIFE

What if we all are meant to show up as the purest, most authentic, non-censored, true version of ourselves?

What if we're all caught up with the reality of this 3D world that keeps us too busy to sit with ourselves?

To me, living a true life is as simple as:

> Setting the intention.
> Trusting that it will happen, just like when you order in a restaurant.
> Listening, seeing or feeling the signs.
> Being open for the outcome to look different to how you expected.

If we were all taught to do this from being little humans, then things in this world would look much more uplifting and lighter. It would be a world where nobody felt unheard or unseen because we'd listen to ourselves and rely on our infinite power.

Instead, we make it so much more complicated!

By now, you have seen that I mention the reality of my life, including the life-changing belief that we're all part of something bigger beyond our comprehension. Some people call it Force, some the Divine, some the Universe, some God, Allah, Krishna... I just know that this infinite powerful part of myself is the same part that makes me feel a deeper and more meaningful connection with everything.

What I've found in this lifetime so far and what I'm exhilarated to show you through this book are the keys to bringing out that inner light of yours and connecting it with your outer self! The ability to reflect on the outside what is going on inside and vice versa is the whole point; living a true life means letting the inner side of you feel positively affected by the choices you make every day, including when it comes to getting dressed.

THE POWER OF SELF-EXPRESSION

There's a therapeutic aspect to all this style game we're learning to play here. You might not have realised it before, but dressing in a way that makes you feel connected to your vision of yourself holds you in an upbeat state. It pushes you to move into that state, even for a minute. The trick is making it a habit.

Creating a closet aligned with your envisioned ideal self sets the foundation for an invaluable reminder of the possibilities open to you.

To put it another way, you can have in front of you every day a snippet of what it's like to be the ideal version of yourself by dressing as your ideal self would.

Can you guess why I talk so much about the *power of style*? Can you see how, when you create a wardrobe from that place of connection, the effects on the outside *can't* be the same as before? Can you see how, if you're able to tap into that vision of yourself and translate it into clothes, you're taking inspired action towards your life's ideal vision? *No matter what you wear.* You're the only one who can do this for yourself.

YOUR SACRED TEMPLE

What I'm about to share with you had a big massive impact on my life and my awareness of the love I have towards my body.

I've always said to my clients, "Your body is your house, your sacred temple, so treat it like what it is."

Don't just ignore that you live inside your body. I never got it myself until I practised this simple exercise.

Style Power Practice:
SENSE YOUR SACRED TEMPLE

Close your eyes and breathe in and out deeply three times. Forget about the outside noise for a minute.

Feel the sensation of being inside of your body. Forget about labels. Nothing bothers you from the outside. Tap into the sensation of peace and comfort inside of yourself.

You might say, "But I'm in pain" or "I don't feel connected to my body". And that's fine. Do yourself a favour and let go. Close your eyes and feel the sensations inside your temple. It's sacred, and you are a miracle. Try to feel every part of your body. Notice your heartbeat and how your breathing flows.

This is a powerful method to love your body more as well as up-levelling the connection with it to give it what it needs. No matter how it looks. You don't even need to like what you see in the mirror, but if you don't fully love your body and project love to it, how are you going to "decorate it" and feed it in the most perfect way?

Since you're reading this, you're probably a person who appreciates beauty in different forms. Maybe you have a picture of the perfect house, or maybe you already live in your ideal place. You love that perfect house, don't you? You treat it nicely. You choose the most beautiful furniture for it.

So, how about your body? How would you treat a body you loved? What kind of food would you put into it? What kind of thoughts would you feed your brain? How would you decorate the facade? Do you want your outside to align with the inside or just choose clothes that are nothing to do with who you are?

Let's go back to imagining that perfect house. Can you imagine a traditional house decorated in black steel and glass? That might be amazing or weird or terrible, depending on those who live in it and how it represents them.

Okay, now let's look at your body in the same way. How do you see it in your dreams? Does it reflect on the outside who you are on the inside?

Here's the thing. We live our lives unconsciously saying, "When I have that house, I'll be happy..." and "When I make

$1 million a year, I'll be happy…" and "When I lose five kilos, I'll be happy…" without realising that being the person who does those things is your choice. Instead of letting outside circumstances take you away from your vision, what if you lived your life *bei*ng the person you see in your wildest dreams?

What if getting dressed, buying clothes and putting together outfits could help you push through the barriers that keep you from living your true purpose?

HEALING PROPERTIES OF YOUR MIND-BODY CONNECTION

Who am I? Have you asked yourself this question lately? After becoming a mum to my second child and going through some of the most challenging times in my lifetime, that one question kept getting stuck in my head. Who am I?

And I'm still figuring it out. I don't think we ever completely answer that question in a lifetime, not in every sense, because our perceptions change as we evolve, and so does our conception of being. There are so many aspects!

Depending on who you ask, they'll answer with their job position, name, family status… I'm a mum, a wife, a daughter, a sister, a style coach, a transformational coach, an empowerment coach, a lover, a friend, a passionate, a creative… So many aspects to it. That's as of today, but that's definitely not all of it!

To get through my almost two-year-long postnatal depression, I drilled into my brain: "I'm healthy." It took me a long time to truly believe it, and so my choices always depended on: If I'm feeling well, *then* I can... If my body can handle it, then I will...

And to be honest, having that depressive battle inside my head for two years did cause some patterns that were tough to get rid of, like the need to remove myself from tantrum situations with my kids as I couldn't face my own internal battle, like having constant self-shame for not being able to operate normally as a mother because most days I could barely get out of bed.

When I finally was able to self-diagnose it (after seeing a gazillion specialists) as some kind of chronic fatigue syndrome, I felt relief. Now I wasn't *just* depressed. I was officially tired for a reason.

As humans, we seek validation, and that's what that diagnosis gave me: reassurance to dig deeper into this new challenge or *gift*, as I'm now discovering.

After a time, the blood tests were looking better, and my adrenals were recovering. (It had been first diagnosed as adrenal fatigue.) Yet still, I couldn't for the love of God move a finger. I wanted to leave my head, even the earth at some points. Some days, I couldn't even get myself dressed. I just couldn't handle the constant state of sadness and depression. However, the days I forced myself to get dressed and put on some makeup, acting and behaving as if I was a fully healthy person, helped tremendously.

Having clothes in my closet that would make me happy if I was in an optimal state of mind helped me reconnect with who I was but couldn't grasp on those long days of crying and low self-worth.

When I look back now, I'm in awe of what we, as a family, went through. The day I came back from an appointment with an Ayurvedic doctor who told me he could cure me for good, I cried a lot because this was the first person who didn't even hint at the fact that I was just depressed and needed to wait, that I should take pills to get through it, that I should stay silent with no answer, or – the one that infuriated me the most – that it was time for me to enjoy my kids and not worry about work because they grow up so fast (as if women couldn't do *both*). Internally, I wondered, *if my husband came here with the same problem, would you tell him the same?* The Ayurvedic doctor, Dr Naveen, simply said, "I feel responsible for your health, and I'm going to heal you." I trusted, and he did.

After my treatment, however, it was up to me to heal myself. How long was I willing to carry that sick identity? That I was sick had become an unconscious belief. In bed one morning, I opened my eyes, and it clicked! I'd been checking what was *wrong* with me every morning on waking and trying to mentally prepare myself for the day ahead, hoping I'd have energy, hoping I'd make it to the end of the day. It had become a habit, but that habit belonged to a sick person who was waiting to fall back into extreme fatigue.

I decided I wasn't going to be that person anymore. It was time to use my auditing experience and take back my power. I would take inventory of a different kind – one where I gathered my energy, stopped fighting my body and listened to it instead!

Since I made the shift to thinking like a healthy person, it has been a domino effect. From that point on, my thoughts were, "I'm a healthy person who sometimes gets tired like everybody else". Now, if I have days when my body tells me I'm tired, I don't make it mean anything. I just ask for help and go lie down. Simple, no shame, no guilt, no resentment.

I keep thinking how many women don't give themselves that free pass, how many of us live trapped in that shame and don't honour where their bodies are. In this hectic, busy, over-worked 3D reality, it's apparently become a shameful declaration to slow down and listen to our bodies, to be less busy or not busy at all. And then we wonder how our bodies can rebel in such a way to demand our attention!

Let me tell you, that same body is the one who can lift you up when you treat it well and decorate it with the utmost care by listening to it. Take it from someone who's healthy and fabulous by choice!

Now I talk to my body, I'm in a relationship with it, and I ask my cells to heal. When you're able to tune in and listen to your cells, the amount of power that you reclaim is breathtaking.

Every day, I say to my body, "Cells, I command you to… so I can…"

Every day, I feel what colour of light flows through my body, starting from the crown of my head down to my feet. That colour tweaks my energy, so the cells of my body all work towards whatever I ask. They answer me. It's sooooo cool! After that, I perceive energy coming from my heart into all my cells, first gratitude, then love.

It feels so good to leave behind the victim role when it comes to health. This is my new empowered self-healing. I'm still learning this new way of life, but boy oh boy, the simple shift of talking and listening to our body is available to all of us.

This method is working for me. Another method might work better for you. Whatever you choose, it should make you feel 100% aligned. The point here is to reclaim *your* power and connection to your sacred temple in all ways! It is you who defines the roadmap to your own empowerment. I'm just here to support that with your clothes.

Most days, when I tune in and ask my body what colour it feels like, it will be the same colour I intuitively choose to wear that day. Trust your body to communicate with you because your body knows.

YOGA IN THIS INNER-CONNECTING JOURNEY

I used to be a bootcamp, extreme exercise type of girl. I still am. However, after going through my adrenal fatigue episodes, that type of extreme exercise was not the only option I was willing to look at anymore.

I first dug into yoga in my years in Toronto pre-kids, but while I enjoyed the practice, I never experienced the deeper meaning of it. It was when I slowly picked it up after recovering from my fatigue phase that I realised how much of the deeper meaning I had missed the first time around. Just like I tell you about style!

And now I see it was meant to be this way. One of my mentors taught me that the reason we get sick or have pain is to do with our body and mind having an argument. At the point where I began talking to my body and being able to sense from the inside of it, I started listening to my body too and practising with more intention. I'm still learning every day this new language of understanding what my body is asking for, what foods it needs, what type of exercise, what choices it wants me to make and what energies it wants me to follow… It's a muscle to flex, just like I tell you about practising mindfulness when it comes to style and connecting with yourself.

Now during yoga, I practise mindfulness and make a conscious decision to connect to my senses. I find it no coincidence that during the period when I reconnected with yoga I also found just the right teachers to encourage this more connected type of life. Like Julio, one of my yoga instructors, who magically channels divine energy when teaching. (You can just feel when an offering is created to serve others and put divine action in place.) In this journey of connecting with myself and realising how it's all connected, practising different yoga versions and opening my body to receive has been key. The practice of namaste – realising how the light in me honours that light in you – was a major shift in my whole system.

I see my style practise, just as I see yoga: the light in me honouring that light in you. By teaching you the Style Power Formula and helping you bring that light of yours out, it shines brighter than ever.

ASK YOUR BODY

Whenever he needs to make a decision, my six-year-old, Tom, closes his eyes and asks his body for the answers, without worrying or being concerned about doing it in front of others. One year on my saint day (something we celebrate in Spain), he went to the shops with Tomás to choose a pair of earrings for me.

While he was there, he saw some cookies and said to the cashier, "I'd like some blue heart cookies, please." The woman in the store replied, "There aren't any blue hearts. There are only blue stars and pink hearts."

With that answer, Tom closed his eyes and said, "Okay, let me check with my body." After a moment, he enthusiastically said, "I'd like the pink heart cookies, four of them."

"Do you know they cost $5?" the woman confused and surprised by Tom's decision making, asked, looking at Tomás, disregarding the 6-year-old's decision.

Tomás looked to Tom as though he was the one in charge and said to the cashier, "Whatever he said."

How on earth could we ever put doubt on my son's capacity to listen to his body like that? He's only six years old but already experiencing the power of having a flowing and reassuring relationship with his body. He does the same when he needs to choose a pair of shoes or an outfit.

That's something I wasn't taught in school. I'm still learning to develop the language of asking my body now.

I'm making sure my kids learn to master it and at the same time, I'm mesmerised by how many signs I receive from the Universe showing me how this game works. It's all about listening to our body, having that deep connection with it, feeling divinely inspired, letting our inner child take over and having fun choosing clothes that make us feel good. No matter what.

We could call it a beautiful kind of occupational therapy, where you isolate yourself from any head chatter and depressive thoughts you might be having and decide to show up for your body and yourself.

Whatever you want to call this power, I'm not willing to contradict my highly intuitive six year old. This stuff is powerful, and we can make it a revolution in listening to our body and dressing in a way that helps us reclaim our power from the inside.

FOOD IS MEDICINE

We've talked about feeding your mind, feeding your soul, but how about your physical body?

As a good Spanish woman, I love food. In Spain, eating and drinking is our social *thing*. We love gathering to eat and drink, which is why when we become parents, it may become such a shock not being able to go out as we please!

I come from a family house where food was the number one investment. My mum would never look at the price when it came to food. Buying the best products was always her priority, and I've totally followed in her footsteps. It wasn't until we moved to Canada that I started to dig deeper into the power of food on my own and the importance of eating unprocessed food.

Most importantly, when I was trying to heal from my chronic fatigue phase, I directly felt the massive effects on brain clarity from eating ridiculous amounts of vegetables and fruits.

As my mum has always said, what you eat is what you are. We used to have a good diet at home. Living abroad, I realised my diet could be improved 10 times to increase my energy levels.

Now, I don't believe one size fits all when it comes to food. Each person has their own DNA, body and blood type, so each person has a different diet that will suit their body. But what I do 100% believe is that eating fresh produce as organic as possible and staying away from all processed fats and sugar, that's the way to go.

I have friends who say, "You're going to die anyway." Of course, that's the *only* thing we know for sure! However, I do have a say in the kind of life I live, and I want that to be the highest quality possible for my family and me, which is why a big chunk of our monthly income goes towards food.

If you're wondering what other ways you could increase your self-worth, try giving your body the food and nutrients it deserves. Treat it like a palace, and you'll feel like gold. Treat like garbage, and… you know what you'll feel.

In my opinion, we don't teach the important correlations between gut and brain well enough. The reason I went through such a long depression after giving birth for the second time was because my gut was out of order. I couldn't absorb nutrients, so of course, I had zero energy! When your gut isn't strong enough because there's no proper balance, parasites and bacteria overgrowth come into the picture, and that's *not* a situation you want to be in, trust me!

To best reflect your inner self on the outside, eat your vegetables, eat your fruit and do your best to eat unprocessed food if you want to have a bright mind and honour your body how it deserves.

I eat to stay healthy, not to stay thin. This is important. I love food. In this house, everyone does! I love cooking. It's my self-expression zone every day. (Unless I'm expected to cook. Then I don't like it. Classic.) Eating to stay thin would cut out one of my ways of enjoying life with my family.

In the end, it's all related. When we eat the best diet for our bodies, a diet that keeps us healthy and happy, we also achieve our ideal weight; when we come to terms with whatever that is and appreciate it for what it is, we've found what's perfect for us.

If you do decide you need to lose weight, focus on *releasing* rather than *losing* weight; otherwise your body will find it again. Ultimately, 'everything in moderation' works well, as long as you're listening to your body.

Treat it like the sacred temple that it is.

STYLE AS FOOD

You know those amazing weekly meal plans where you can shop for groceries and batch cook for the whole week? They don't work for me, because to me cooking is a way to express myself, just like dressing. I love having my pantry full of goodies, just like I love having my wardrobe full of pieces I simply adore, and then I can let my inspiration take over on the day. Some people could eat the same food every day as long as they didn't have to think about what to eat. I, on the other end, can't have the same dinner two days in a row. The same goes for clothes.

And look, I get it. It's not like you *can't* thrive with the right clothes! Take Steve Jobs, for example. One of the most popular anecdotes about him is how he always wore basically the same clothes to eliminate the daily decision of what to wear and free up the space it took up in his head. But using the analogy of food again, I love *enjoying* it and I love *having fun* cooking new creations with what I have in my kitchen. Could I thrive eating the same food every day? There's no unicorn way because that doesn't feed my soul! It doesn't bring me joy.

I want to broaden the narrow concept of style as a simple matter of putting on nice clothes, spending money lavishly on pieces of fabric, looking at it as an extension of the superficial fashion industry. The point is I love enjoying my food as much as I love enjoying, having fun and feeling a connection with what I wear.

Of course, perhaps you could go the Steve Jobs way if being strategic feels and looks good to you. Once you do the work that I'll give you and have the tools to systemise the hell out of your wardrobe (I see you A types!), you might fancy being a Steve Jobs every single day in your life, but your own version!

I believe that the way we dress supports our inner-outer connection.

I believe it goes from the inside-out at first, not so much from the outside-in when you're at the beginning of practising a new way of being. Once we discover our light and have that feeling of connection, there's no going back. Dressing is a reflection of our inner selves. You show up in accordance with who you are.

When you're able to make that connection and identify those pieces that'll start creating that feeling of connection within you, then we can start talking on a deeper level about the outside-in effect. That outside-in effect is undeniable, and there are several studies to support it.

In 2012, a study published by professors at Kellogg School of Management at Northwestern University introduced the term "enclothed cognition" to describe the systematic influence that clothes have on the wearer's psychological processes.

In 2013, Professor Karen Pine of the University of Hertfordshire found women neglect 90% of their wardrobe when under stress. All the research she did around clothing showed how people's mental processes and perceptions could be primed by clothing, as they internalise the symbolic meaning of what they're wearing.

I'm telling you this not to put pressure on you, but to uplift you! In the beginning, it's completely normal if you feel you're not doing it *right* (as if there was a right or wrong!), but that's just not true. I *love* when I see my clients getting it *wrong* because it's a sign that they're pushing boundaries and experimenting with feeling uncomfortable in new-to-them combinations!

Clothes can be a tool for you to thrive or not. It's a matter of choice. What do you want them to mean for you?

SET YOUR MESSAGE FREE

What if I told you that you can speak with your appearance, clothes, makeup and hair? What if I told you, if you're a person who's having a hard time getting your message across, that you can align your outer appearance with your message and make your actions 10 times more effective? This means genuinely coming from that light of yours. Being able to reflect your innate personality and gifts is liberating.

It's a golden chance to show up authentically, and there are no rules.

Nowadays, if I don't feel that the way I'm dressing shows some part of me, I feel empty, unseen.

And it's easy for me to activate that invisible mode. As you'll see in the coming pages, I spent *years* mastering that mode of being. But even during those years at school where I truly wanted to disappear, I always managed to catch the attention of those bullies… I wasn't making any noise or doing any harm, but somehow they'd see me and find an excuse to direct their actions towards me.

I'd wonder why, but I see it now. Even if we don't believe in that powerful light or want to hide it, which I always knew was there, we always trigger those who aren't willing to grow like we are. And that's okay.

They didn't know better, and for that, I don't hold anything against those souls. For starters, because I also hurt others with my actions. And boy, did it take me some time to truly get over that story of why so many people "hated me", as I'd say at the time.

Now I live from a very different place. It came to me while I was cooking one day over Easter. Just like my mum used to, I was cooking up a storm for the whole family to enjoy together on Easter Day, and suddenly I realised I let go of an important barrier that was keeping me from allowing and receiving. I now accept all love into my life and keep track of it in my receiving journal. I allow that love to do all the good it can in me, because there's no bigger, purer and more magnificent energy than the energy of love.

So there I was, cooking in the kitchen, crying and releasing what I'd been holding onto all this time: I'd let others' mostly negative opinions shape my life and block me from my true path.

That day, I saw clearly how instead of allowing that powerful and unconditional love to fill me with its goodness, I'd been blocking it! Somehow, I hadn't felt worthy of that love.

Yet again, I'd found self-connection through food creation, and it allowed me to see the light.

LETTING GO OF THE RULES

What if the answer to getting unstuck in your style situation was you? What if the answer to getting to the next level of who you want to be was you? What if you had the answer? What if you just need to dig deeper into who you really are and the rest of the process will unfold? What if it could be effortless, just like that?

Only one condition. You will let go of expectations that things need to look one way or the other for you to receive them. And it'll be like learning how to ride a bike. Once you have the formula in your head, you won't need me or this book until your next phase in life, where you might want to revisit and apply this process again to the new version of yourself.

As you will see, the style tools that I show you later on in the book will evolve as you evolve. We'll stay away from the old and boring style rules, and we'll create the foundation for you to paint your own picture, using the right tools and your body as the blank canvas.

The **Style Power Formula** might look overly simple to some, but it's the exact process I apply to style nowadays and nothing else.

I wanted to leave overwhelm outside of this book and set your imagination free so that you have power to determine how you show up and what you can achieve in your personal life, work and business life... Starting from the most important connection, you need to nurture if you want the style of your dreams, the connection you have with yourself and your intuition.

After you read this book, if you feel like you're craving more style rules because you've become hooked on this style game, I understand, and I have more resources on my website. But let me tell you this: the Style Power Formula is more than a head start; the Style Power Formula is the whole game. I'm about to open the door to all my secrets of how you can show up every day with confidence and pride to be fully yourself.

PROJECTION AND SELF-CONNECTION

Each son has changed me in unexpected ways. My kids are my greatest teachers, the ones who've created the foundations of the real evolved me. I used to get angry at just about anything in my life. Then one day, when my eldest was five, I decided to visualise in hypnosis what would happen if I was at peace all the time no matter what.

The peaceful vision wasn't realised in a matter of days or weeks. It took months of audio hypnosis programming and *seeing* myself feeling at peace in my mind's eye. But I see now how that the habit of anger was creating a major disconnection with myself and with my kids. I felt I was failing myself every day and had an unbearable feeling of guilt and shame for being so far from the perfect mother I wanted to be.

When the Covid-19 pandemic arrived and I realised I was going to be at home full time with my two boys all day, I experienced the peace I had been envisioning for the first time. I had no fear. I wasn't afraid of what was coming. It was pure peace. In fact, I only realised that this peace had finally come to me when I raised my voice one day, and Tom replied, "Mummy, I think you're tired. It's been a hard day."

That I allowed myself to forgive myself for all the anger I'd projected in the past, but also acknowledge that screaming and losing it was not an everyday ordeal at home anymore. I thought I was supposed to be home-schooling my kids during the pandemic, but they were the ones teaching me life lessons.

You can feel sad, tired or down, and still live in a constant state of joy and peace. When you decide to take your hand off the wheel and allow your divine light to tell you how to drive, you can trust that you are guided. It's subtle at first, but if you listen, it'll get easier and easier.

I definitely don't have this all figured out. We all have our days. But when we live life from that proactive and surrendered state, life happens for us, everything is a lesson, and we can feel grateful for it.

ON BEING HARD ON YOURSELF AND SURRENDER

There's so much we don't know. There're so many mysteries that we just can't solve. When I'm all philosophical, I imagine how this world is just *The Matrix* with all this information in the background that we're completely oblivious of. (There are no coincidences when you know my favourite singer is NE-YO.) The power of uncertainty and being at peace with it is called *surrender*.

I realised not long ago that surrender was key to letting go of all the stress I was experiencing in my life after having little ones. Trying to be like any other mother was and still is pointless. I see it now.

Trying to compare to the standards of the ideal picture you see on the outside. Those amazing women entrepreneurs with a gazillion kids and a multimillion-dollar business always looking fit and healthy.

How do we get ourselves lost in comparison to non-existent ideals? We look at others' lives thinking we'd like what they have, but are we willing to give up our three-hour-per-night TV habit? Are we willing to give up those sweets? How about time with the family or the sense of being responsibility-free?

In an interview with Oprah, Lady Gaga explained how much physical pain she had been going through and how she had hidden it so well from the outside that we could only see the tip of the iceberg. Oprah pointed out that so many people would want Lady Gaga's life, but if they wanted it, they'd need to take it all.

There's always a side that we don't see, and 99% of people's reality isn't shared on social media. However, we tend to fill in the blanks. We imagine what our ideal would look like, then from that perfect picture, we compare our everyday life to it and end up feeling like we aren't good enough or like we've failed. We need to stop creating our dreams based on what we think others have or do.

The Covid-19 pandemic was a unique time of surrender and embracing imperfection. TV time? No shame. Being in activewear all day? No shame. Screaming? Reset, say sorry and move on.

Aiming for perfection would have added too much pressure during the pandemic, given the uncertainty and messiness there was on the outside. Personally, I embraced the fact that we are also allowed to lose it sometimes, and that's okay, as long as we're responsible for it and see it as a sign to take care of ourselves. Our kids get angry and scream when their hunger or tiredness knocks on the door, and we always understand that, so why don't we do this with our own needs?

Claiming this and sharing it with my children has taken a huge weight off my shoulders. I'm no longer searching for perfection, giving myself such a hard time or seeking validation, just looking for connection in that moment. And that's okay, no matter how messy some days look.

WELCOME TO THE WORLD

Hopefully, through this pillar, you've become more familiar with the perspectives you need to cultivate a sense of self. One last question before we dive into the roadmap to feeling empowered in your style. What if you're meant for more? It's time to stop delegating to others what you want. You know, deep down, what ignites your light.

Welcome to a world of colour and endless possibility. Before you enter this technicolour paradise, know that everything I'm sharing with you are vision and identity tools that have helped me move towards who I really am; they're not style rules for you to follow blindly in an all-time boring pattern. No!

Are you ready to make that inner-outer connection happen? This is an opportunity to give yourself permission to let your soul lead the way and release 3D labels like age, social status, locations and expectations. Let's create that vision and step into a new style of being.

PILLAR TWO

Roadmap to Style Empowerment

WHATEVER YOU CAN SEE IN YOUR MIND, KNOW THAT IT ALREADY EXISTS. NOW IT'S JUST A MATTER OF TRUST.

In this second part of the Style Power Formula, I'm introducing you to the bridge from the inside-out work to the "outside-in" work. I'm going to help you tap into possibility and what it is that you're actually made for. And only from that space, we'll be able to diagnose what stands between this moment and the vision you will see for yourself.

STYLE POWER

CHAPTER THREE

Creating your empowered vision*

DEALING WITH INSECURITIES

"I'm powerful, I'm so powerful." I drill that into my brain as I keep pushing forward on the limit I set myself, the limit that tells me I'm not good enough. And then when the logical mind comes in, it says: "But you aren't *that* smart, or *that* gifted, or *that* brave."

Yes, all day. Every day, I keep hearing these voices. The question is: what is *that* enough? What exactly is *that* level where we stop questioning ourselves? Is there even a ladder to compare where we stand?

That is the pattern interruption I use when getting into the downward spiral. I choose to be smart, trained, gifted, magical and beautiful right now, and stop the rest of the mind clutter.

When are you going to allow the real light to come through you? Because there's a reason you're here. Out of trillions of possibilities, time, people, chances and even sperm, everything came together so that you are here.

Some people are brave enough to keep searching. They believe they're here for a reason, *the* reason. Who knows what our real reason is? God knows.

The only thing I know is what feels warmer brings me closer to my light. That's what I follow now. I set an intention at the start of writing this book to finish it while attracting money effortlessly and focusing only on serving. For a recovered, self-sabotage, scarcity-mentality woman, this was a big stretch but finally the time came when I said, "Enough. It can't be this hard. Life can't be this hard. What if I tried at 37, as a mother, wife, daughter, friend and proud woman to let go once and for all and just trust?"

Set the intention and then start taking inspired action. Minute by minute. Day by day. There's paradise on the other side, and you can trust that.

THE WAKE-UP CALL

I believe that one of the reasons the 2020 pandemic happened for me specifically was to stop pretending style was a lavish, superficial game to "sell my message" and once and for all "come out of the closet" making public how much deeper I've always worked with style.

I mean, how was I going to talk about what type of jeans to buy when everybody was worried about their security, their jobs and trying to handle being at home with the kids?

By talking about the therapeutic aspect of clothes, and how wearing certain colours and styles at home helped me feel more connected to myself and not *lose it*, this whole style game could take a new perspective, right?

It was a time to dig deeper and live in the now, coming out as the spiritual style expert I've always been. And how do I know that? Well, as soon as I came clean about who I truly was, those people who followed me for years said, "Duh, of course that's what your message has always been."

Sometimes we resist a change that, in reality, was already obvious to everyone but ourselves. That's what I call getting in our own way. It takes a wake-up call, like for me, the pandemic, to realise what actually matters to us.

So, I ask you to stop and ask yourself, "How can I make life easy? How can I follow the flow?"

JUST CLOTHES

One day as I was brewing this book, I was explaining to my friends how I needed to bring out this message about style being far more than just about clothes. Style was so much more to me. In fact, I was worried that people would perceive getting dressed as *just about clothes* and not see the deeper meaning behind it.

As soon as I started writing, all these random people appeared in my life to deliver me messages I've *never* received in the past:

Stop saying it's just clothes. That isn't true!
This is about so much more.
You're giving others the opportunity to grow in major ways.
This is something we put on our bodies every day. It is energy. Everything is energy.

I don't believe I started attracting all these random messengers for no reason. I believe they came to me because my message needed to get out. And this is the next step on that road to empowerment: sharing your deeper message through style.

Once, I heard spiritual author and motivational speaker Wayne Dyer say we should do more 'as Christ on earth' rather than following the dogma of Christianity.

This really spoke to me because God moves with unconditional love. He believes in me. He is the one pulling me towards sharing this message. I decided I had to get this message out.

What you wear is more than just clothes. It's an expression of who you are. Even for me, this feels unreal sometimes, but I've been in the image industry for so long and been exposed to all this self-development and spiritual wisdom that I know this marriage of the two is needed. My message brings together style and spiritual wisdom. Creatively speaking, this message is my baby.

THE PERSONAL SHOPPING TRAP

I believe we all have an upgraded version of ourselves within, and I'm great at seeing it in every single person. I'm not so great at accepting that not everybody wants to move towards it or even believes they can. I try to accept it, but it's a challenge to stop myself from shaking those I work with and tell them: wake up!

Instead, I stop and accept the fact that the best way to honour them is to accept their divine timing and go above and beyond to show them the way.

I'm a "tell it like it is" kind of woman. Honesty is a high value for me. It always has been; telling you otherwise wouldn't make sense. I've polished myself through the years and developed my empathy too, only because I realised I deserved to hear it myself first, before connecting with others on their level.

So, let me say this straight. Working in image consulting, I don't believe I'm here to buy people clothes and get them wearing those clothes. I *thought* that was my calling until I did it, and it felt off.

What I see when I look at you isn't what you see in the mirror. I see you at your highest potential, and I believe my dharma is to help you see that for yourself too and start dressing for it. (That's where I come in!)

At some point in my career, I decided to only assist with the personal shopping part of image consulting with those who had *already* gone through the inner shift. In other words, they had "converted".

I retired from being a Band-Aid style consultant who fixed wardrobe problems from the outside and decided to only serve clients who wanted to work at a deeper level. Needless to say, the transformations I've witnessed since then have been truly magical.

Real transformations start from within, and your expectations are a key factor in that. Nobody knows your body better than you do. By doing this deep work first, you'll realise what I mean!

BUILDING YOUR EMPOWERED STYLE VISION

So, let's talk about that vision you have of yourself, that potential self I've been talking so much about! Only when we've been able to envision it can we create the plan to achieve it.

Before we get to the envisioning exercise, a few guidelines:

1. **The idea is to create a perfect vision without limits.**
   If there were no limits whatsoever, how would you see your ideal self?

2. **Always, always dress for *yourself*. Dress yourself to impress *yourself*.**
   We're our harshest critics, and we need to accept that loving voice inside of us. Even if it doesn't seem like it's there now, I guarantee you it was there when you were born. Listen for the voice of love and acceptance for what you're creating.

3. **You're the priority. Until you love the way you dress and honour your efforts in showing up authentically, you won't be able to reach your vision.**

   You cannot set goals based on somebody else's expectations. You don't have control over anybody else's way of being. The only thing you can control are your own reactions.

When you're able to connect to that personal power and dress to honour yourself, really owning it, your life will start to change because you'll start changing your perspective.

Once you take care of your own business, then you can start helping others with your gifts.

Now, of course, you want to make your loved ones proud, but that won't feel the same if you don't do it from a place of alignment with your truest light!

Okay, so let's create that vision of yours.

Style Power Practice:
ENVISIONING YOUR IDEAL SELF

Sit with a blank page in front of you and connect with your heart. Place your hands over your heart, feel your heartbeat and breathe three times. Now ask it what the ultimate expression of your highest and most expansive self would look like. You should hear an answer while connected to your heart centre.

Get quiet and tune into that version of you that's 100% aligned with your highest self.

With an ideal version of yourself clear in your mind, let's set that light of yours free by imagining yourself at work (whatever that is for you) in a year from now. If you work from home, imagine you have an event, or you have an important meeting. You've evolved to new levels. See how you feel in that situation.

Confident? Powerful? Effective? With a voice? At peace?

Now write down what you experience. Write down what you see, how you talk, who you're interacting with and how you feel when you talk to them.

Also, notice what you wear. How are you feeling when you wear it? How do you feel others are perceiving you? Does it matter to you what others say? Who are you dressing for? If you can't picture it, don't fixate upon it.

If your clothing style stays the same as it is now, don't worry about old-fashioned looks. Just go with what it feels like. Many people who live in the present time are inspired by 1920s fashion, for example, so there are no limits to your imagination.

If your clothing style is different to what you wear now, what style is it? What colour? How do you feel about it?

Notice how much money you seem to be making. How big are you? When I say big, I don't mean in terms of body size, money or fame. I mean, look at your level of expansion, however you measure that. In your vision, see yourself at the biggest level of expansion you can imagine. Don't limit yourself.

If you're more a kinesthetic or auditory person, don't worry about visuals, go with whatever your natural sensing tendency is.

REMEMBER: THERE ARE NO LIMITS. LITERALLY ANYTHING IS POSSIBLE.

Feel that expanded sensation in your body. Now pause there and answer this:

Are you made for more?
Are you made for infinite potential?
Are you ready to get over the stories in your head of not being good enough?
Are you ready to get your wardrobe sorted and live your life from that place every single day for the rest of your life?

Next, think about people you admire in terms of how they dress or how they carry themselves. It can be family, friends, acquaintances, celebrities alive or dead, decades of fashion. Write down what you love about how each person dresses or carries themselves. Why do you think that captures your attention? What is this mirroring for you?

Next, imagine clothes you love and have always loved or types of clothes that were "so you". They might be in your closet currently. They might not. Write down what you love about them.

How about colours? What are your favourite and least favourite colours, and why?

In your vision, notice your level of confidence both in how you show up and how you create your dream outfits by yourself. If you see it, it's within you. Believe it. Embrace it.

With all the answers you've written down, what are some patterns you've observed? What's your ultimate goal? What's your ultimate feeling? What's your ultimate empowered style vision?

You've done some great work, so it's time for us to use it and put it into practice. In the next chapter, we're going to keep nailing your very own Style Power Formula that you've already been working on.

WHATEVER YOU DO, KEEP MOVING FORWARD

An important part of getting to your ideal self that you've just envisioned is to keep moving. Through inspired action, we make things happen.

I love that feeling of momentum when you find that sweet spot of your style, decide how you want to show up and start putting the pieces together. If you're at that point, don't stop! Taking action now is the most important thing you can do because if you stop, your ideal self will never become a reality.

By creating momentum and taking consistent action, you'll put together a closet that reminds you what you're capable of every single morning when you get dressed. How's that for a good start to your day?

CHAPTER FOUR

Spotting your identities *

IDENTITY IN YOUR LIFE

An identity is the set of beliefs we hold about ourselves that dictates the way we behave. Ultimately, this will determine our life. Unfortunately, our identity usually comes entangled in crappy unconscious beliefs that will determine how we perceive our reality.

When you first get this, you may feel like you're discovering the matrix because you realise your reality is no more than a number of interpretations of what you see and that you can change them anytime you want as long as you're aware of them.

Here are some examples of how my identity has got in the way of me moving forward, starting with writing this book.

In the past I held the belief that writing a book wasn't something I should do because I wasn't 'good enough' to share my knowledge. Okay, let's dismantle this amount of crap:

- What makes me think I'm not good enough?
- When will enough be enough?
- What am I gaining by thinking this way?

- If my identity doesn't include confidence in sharing my message and honouring my dharma, then how am I ever going to feel fulfilled?

Now let's apply this to style.

Let's say I have the belief that I'm 'too fat' to wear something. Maybe I think, *what are people going to say*? I completely disregard the fact that I *love* the item and would *love* to wear it. Right, let's dismantle this incredibly popular one. If I hold the belief that I'm fat, what am I including into my every day?

- What makes me think I'm less than?
- Less than what?
- I can't do XYZ because...?
- I can't wear ABC because...?
- I can't do diets because...?

All I see there are *limitations*, but this book is all about setting yourself free, so let's look at transforming this identity.

Just to be clear, I hate this word – fat. So, what if we threw that fat identity out of the window? What if, instead of fat, we started feeling FAT, as in Flawless, Achieving and Toned. That's another interpretation of the same letters. With this interpretation, the way we'd act would be totally different.

- We're no more and no less than anyone else. We are just ourselves. (Every culture has a different idea of what *fat* means anyway, so why would you determine your culture to influence your life?)
- We can wear whatever makes us happy because it's perfect for us.

- We can eat healthily and take care of our body because we love it, and we want to live a long life to make the impact we came to this world to make.

Yes, the identity you hold about yourself will influence the way you approach every single thing in your life: social life, love life, food, clothes, work, sex… Every single thing!

So, take a minute and reflect on what *word* is limiting you.

How about we look into a system that can make you aware of the identity you're holding about yourself and shift it? It sounds pretty natural to shift into our best identity *before* we start looking at the best ways to dress.

How do you know what beliefs you're telling yourself? If you're an over-doer like I was, you might cringe, but the way I became aware of my identities was by being silent, doing nothing. Like nothing for four hours. Yup, that's right. Just me and my thoughts. We live in a culture of keeping ourselves busy so that we don't give our amazingly creative brains a chance to listen to our thoughts.

Even though you might call yourself positive and optimistic (like I used to), stop for a sec and start noticing what your inner talk looks like on your everyday basis.

THE S.T.Y.L.E. IDENTITY METHOD™

I created this method for you to discover your personal pattern when it comes to choosing what to wear every morning and to uncover the reason why you feel stuck when it comes to finding the flow in your style.

It's time for you to start showing up just as you pictured yourself in your vision exercise, get to know yourself better so that you can dress the best for you, and better yet, increase your awareness to understand how to up-level your style. Best of all, it's based on my number one belief that nobody knows your body better than you.

This is about recalling your power and realising how much your clothes can be a sign of what's standing between where you are right now and where you want to be.

Our inner-outer connection is fundamental for us to feel "in the zone".

> If you value beauty and enjoy looking good...
>
> If you want to be the best at being you and to discover what it is that sets you apart from the masses...
>
> If being authentic and helping others is something you believe you're here for...
>
> If you want to live your life to the fullest, learn how to be more present with your family and those around you, as well as taking your business or work life to the next level...

Start right now unveiling your S.T.Y.L.E. Identity and how you can make the most of it to look just like you did in the vision you just built in the last chapter.

You can do this all by yourself, with me in your pocket. You take all the credit, and we both get personal satisfaction when you open the door to unlimited self-growth (while looking pretty amazing).

Our identity dictates the way we hold our self-concept. This identity we carry will direct the way we behave, the choices we make and our perceptions in life.

When you're being the person you want to be, your behaviour will align with that. If you're a healthy person (and hold the identity of a healthy person), your daily food choices and automatic habits will probably be very different than if you hold the identity of an overeater or a proud junk food consumer. And it's the same with the way we show up in our closet every day.

This S.T.Y.L.E. Identity profile system might also give you some hints on why you feel stuck with your wardrobe and how you can move forward. Here's the thing. The goal of this system isn't for you to switch style identities necessarily, but for you to shift your *awareness* and observe what exactly is the style identity you hold (and the beliefs associated with it) that keep you stuck! That said, as you go through all the profiles, you might feel inclined to switch your identity consciously. It's very possible. You might see yourself moving forward with a new identity and implementing the tips in order to make the most of your style!

Anything goes! Remember: this book is always here for you as you move closer to who you are on all levels.

Notice that this exercise not only increases your awareness of why you may be feeling stuck in your style game, but will apply to all areas of your life.

How you show up in your wardrobe is how you show up in life.

Let's do this!

What's Your Style Identity?

S.T.Y.L.E. is an acronym that stands for five types of identities:

The **S**afe Player who plays safe and doesn't take risks.

The **T**uned-In one who dresses how they *feel* and usually doesn't pay attention to how to combine pieces. Sometimes they nail it.

The **Y**es-er who says yes to everybody. Their wardrobe is packed but they don't know what to wear.

The **L**awbreaker is that rebel without a cause, who is so focused on breaking all the rules that sometimes they are too focused on breaking them and not focused enough on dressing in a way that makes them feel aligned.

The **E**arly Adopter follows fashion trends no matter what, but forgets about an all-important factor: their personality.

One day, as I was meditating in my sacred spot, I somehow knew I needed to create a way to identify what might be standing between you and your empowered style, and these profiles came to me as a way to categorise those subconscious daily patterns in your everyday life, the patterns that make you put together certain outfits, then look in the mirror and feel blah!

Before we talk about external style tools, let's find out what you need to address so that you can show up in a way that makes you feel attractive, seen, worthy of everything you want and beautiful from the inside out.

The way you dress is all embedded in your identity. Increasing your awareness of what you think you are will shed some light and allow you to move forward. Discover what makes you dress in the way you do and how you can start dressing in a way that makes you feel more alive than ever.

There's a reason why you feel stuck, but which reason is it? The following deep-dives into the five S.T.Y.L.E. Identities can help you figure out what areas in your life might need to shift for everything else to fall into place. The way you show up every day in your closet can be an eye-opener to identify why you hit a certain plateau in your life.

Will you dare to dress in a way that's connected to your soul and with the ultimate vision of success that you hold within yourself?

Let's find out which S.T.Y.L.E. Identity is leading you astray in your wardrobe and your life?

*

S - The Safe Player

Hey S! (May I call you S?) You're a sweet soul who lives to make the world a better place, and by world, I mean those who come in contact with you. You always want to help and love being of service to others. Your kindness and beautiful manner makes you a one-of-a-kind even though you hardly see yourself that way.

You know who I'm talking about. It's you who we all love, but maybe you don't want to see it, feel it or receive it.

Now, feeling, this is a big one for you. This is a muscle we can flex and start exploring, can't we? You might be more of a visual person, but I want to tell you that I love you and I see you, and I also *feel* you.

There was a time when I used to hide behind this identity because the only thing I wanted to do was to fit in. But that was a hard task being a 5'6" tall girl in a class of 4 to 5 feet tall boys and girls. At school, I was basically one head taller than the rest of the class, and for somebody who just wanted to fit in, that was devastating. In sixth grade, I went to a new school, a traditional Catholic school and the more I wanted to please others and fit in, the more I'd stand out because my nature wasn't living from this identity.

I was meant to embrace standing out, not hiding, and I see that now. I was meant to own my heart, my beautiful and quirky personality, as well as my clothes instead of trying to fit in.

Why am I telling you this? Because your identity might feel like something you were born with, and you can't change it. It's "just who you are", right? Wrong! At least not true if you use this identity as an excuse to move forward. That's 100% a victim mentality, and we don't play that kind of game around here! Get ready to up-level your game in life starting from right now, my sweet friend.

SAFE PLAYER STYLE PROFILE

You're not comfortable taking risks. You prefer being in your comfort zone, even if that means sacrificing the inner fire that wants to burst with the most magnificent power and peacefully change the world.

As your profile name states, safety is a high value of yours. Feeling safe is something you need to thrive.

Here's a little discovery I made some time ago: safety and security are an illusion. What feels safe for me might be incredibly unsafe for somebody else and vice versa.

You like to follow rules, and you thrive in a predictable environment.

Your style is considered "average", meaning it doesn't stand out, and you're happy with that.

You don't like being the centre of attention and prefer taking care of others and always doing the "right thing".

Dressing in a way that's appropriate to every situation is the one rule you follow every time you decide to put clothes on.

You do have days when you feel more adventurous and try to put on a creative, colourful necklace, but when you see yourself in the mirror or in a photo, it just doesn't work.

And after those failed attempts, you repeat in your head, "I'm just not creative. I'm not meant to dress this way. That was silly of me."

WHAT KEEPS THE SAFE PLAYER STUCK AND FUNKED?

You've invalidated that unique voice inside of you for too long, and now you feel like innovating isn't something that you do. But if you stop and think about it, you weren't born with that limitation. Somewhere, somehow, you learned in your lifetime to quiet your unique impulses and follow only external rules.

This is your opportunity to bring that personal power of yours more to life, in your own way.

The one reason you feel like you're going down a dead-end street when it comes to your wardrobe is that you've lost connection with yourself and to what you really want.

When we keep numbing our urges, it comes to a point where we believe we're just meant to be like everybody else seems to be. Then we feel "stuck", and we look for answers – again outside of ourselves. The only place where you can find the solution is where it all started – on the inside.

The good news? Unlocking this path with your wardrobe will have unlimited knock-on effects that'll positively impact other aspects of your life!

SAFE PLAYER S.T.Y.L.E. IDENTITY SHIFT

Here's the shift you need to make as a Safe Player...

Connect to your heart.

That amazing heart energy you have, what is it saying?

Identify what sets your heart on fire, no matter how ridiculous you think it may seem to others. It is time for you to start living your life outside of other people's expectations.

This is the thing, my dear S. One day, you'll be lying on your death bed about to leave this 3D world, and you won't remember all the times you did "what you were expected to do" or "the popular right thing". You'll remember that prison feeling you got every time you had a hunch telling you to write outside the lines and that little voice inside of you told you not to do it to keep you safe. Even though you had a hunch to start writing on your own terms, you followed that voice in your head because you've always been taught to do the right thing.

In those last breaths, they say your life passes in front of you. In that moment, that same voice will be there to tell you nothing but... *Hey! You're about to die. You probably should've been more you!*

That voice is part of you. We all have it. It's there to keep you safe, giving you the guidelines to live within limits. That voice is your fear – your inner critic – or as I like to call it, your "write within the lines voice".

Right now, you need to embrace your Dora the Explorer and put that voice of yours in your backpack because it's time to live the adventure you came to live, dressed the way you're called to dress. In fact, it's time to leave that backpack behind and create a new one.

That voice isn't the one that will suggest you dress in a way that makes you feel *alive*. Listening to that voice won't get you out of the *funk* you're in.

Now, let's see what you can shift to make your heart sing:

One #1:
CONNECT WITH YOUR HEART

Meditate every day for 10 days in a row, use binaural beats to calm your mind and see what comes up. (Look back to Chapter One if you need more help with tuning in.)

As an S, you can try this mantra during meditation, paraphrasing one of my mentors, Jim Fortin:

No matter what, everything has always been okay, is okay and will always be okay.

When you're able to surrender and trust that is true, magic happens.

Clue #2:
OPEN YOUR ENERGY

Use this style shift question to open your energy:

What would it look like for me to express myself through clothes feeling safe?

Ask yourself this question three times a day and notice what comes up.

Clue #3:
CONNECT YOUR CLOTHES TO YOUR VISION

Go to your closet and identify those pieces that you feel encompass that version of yourself that you built during the vision exercise. Make sure that ideal version of yours feels like it's connected to that highest expression of your essence and dream like nobody's watching. (Oh wait, there's actually nobody watching!)

Once you have that good sense of your ultimate expression, go to your closet and connect to even one piece. Get a good sense of how it makes you feel.

Then, and only then, you're ready to start looking at the upcoming (Un)conventional Style Tools and start designing your way to freedom.

Your beautiful identity is here to keep you safe. Acknowledge it and act from a place of gratitude.

Remember: This isn't an exercise to make your identity right or wrong; it's to help you increase your awareness on how keeping this identity may not only be stopping you from dressing to your highest potential but also showing up in all areas of your life as you're meant to.

SAFE PLAYER Q&A

Q. What if I've got nothing in my closet that's connected to my ideal version of myself?
A. That's okay! If you can set aside a little budget to start buying some pieces following the system in the following chapters, you'll soon be able to connect with some pieces of the empowered vision of you. If you can't afford to buy now, that's okay too. Just start setting the intention. Focus on what you want, live as if you already have it and don't focus on your circumstances. Trust me!

Q. What if I don't want to change and just want to keep playing safe?
A. Then stay! All I want for you is to be happy.

Q. What if I can't meditate? I just can't seem to stop my head!
A. Play binaural beats, do guided or walking meditations, try running or painting; just anything that'll get you out of your mind and into your heart.

Get quiet and the monkey mind will stop at some point. It doesn't have to be perfect. It's just a matter of taking time to sit down and acknowledge yourself. Give yourself the gift of time, this precious but non-existent commodity.

You're worth it.

T - The Tuned-In

My dear T, you're very intuitive and most likely spiritual. You live every day from a place that knows you're not alone in this physical world. There's more to your life than just this 3D existence, and knowing this allows you to take action in a different way than the masses.

You always rely on your inner wisdom to choose what to wear every morning.

You probably do it without even realising, and you've done it this way because you assume everybody gets dressed in the same line of thought. And this couldn't be further from the truth.

Allow your identity to guide you to make the best choices for you, but don't lose sight of the outcome you want for the way you dress. Remind yourself that your vision for yourself is as important as how you feel in this moment.

Just because I think both chocolate and bone broth will feel good in my body doesn't mean I'm going to eat them at the same time. Take this opportunity to be open to the ways your outfits can be created.

TUNED-IN STYLE PROFILE

Dressing your body is yet another way to honour the sacred house or "bag of skin" you were given in this lifetime. By tuning in and checking what feels right to wear today, you're unconsciously infusing your body with an extra dose of self-empowerment and self-honouring of your beautiful soul.

And that, my friend, is 100% shown in your energy. When you learn the language of clothes, it is palpable every single day when you step out of the door. It's the secret to why you project so much magic and peace.

You care a lot about others, and you always look for their highest good. You don't hang out with everyone, just the people with whom you feel a special energetic connection.

You enjoy dressing in a way that expresses your inner self and allows you to set free that inner world of yours that you can hardly explain with words.

Dressing is a form of art, and that's the reason you can do it instinctively.

WHAT KEEPS THE TUNED-IN STUCK AND FUNKED?

You're right on the Style Power path and that might be the reason you felt attracted to this book in the first place. You get the idea of what it is to dress in a way that's 100% connected to who you are.

However, on this path, despite all the right signs, you might get lost admiring the beauty of patterns, textures or special shapes and forget the whole point of getting dressed, which is for your outer self to feel one with your inner self and in harmony with it all.

That's the reason why so many days you look in the mirror and think, *how on earth did that happen?* Or, *what was I thinking?*

TUNED-IN S.T.Y.L.E. IDENTITY SHIFT

I have some amazing news for you: You already live the *tricky* part of the Style Power Formula. Now it's just a matter of using the right tools to dress in a way that allows you to feel pumped every morning with your outfit creations.

Just like a painter has the vision and needs to use the right type of paint and canvas for their art to materialise, so too do you need the right tools to create your own daily masterpiece AKA outfit to fulfil your soul's expression. (I'll give you these in the next section. You'll find your saving grace in Chapter 8!)

In the meantime, here are a few clues to shifting your style identity.

Clue #1:

GROUNDING

Dear T, given your magical nature and ability to live connected to *it all*, you might forget the fact that Mother Earth is here to give you answers too. Ground yourself every day by walking barefoot on the earth (outside if you can) and consciously set the intention to stay connected through your feet. Doing this will give you a good sense of this 3D reality and will help you create the outfits that you want.

Clue #2:

OPEN YOUR ENERGY

Use this style shift question to open your energy:

What would it look like if I could create a style that reflects me in 3D with ease and joy?

Ask yourself this every day until the answer appears.

Clue #3:
ARM YOURSELF WITH STYLE TOOLS

You're on the right path to Style Power. If you arm yourself with the (Un)conventional Style Tools in Chapters 6, 7 and 8, your reward when dressing every morning will be 10 times sweeter.

TUNED-IN Q&A

Q. What if it feels unnatural focusing too much on how I look?

A. This is part of why we're specifying your S.T.Y.L.E. Identity before we move on to focus on the visual aspects of your body.

I have many spiritual friends who used to struggle with the fact that we live in a physical world, and they "had to" deal with 3D stuff. I like to twist things around and look at life from this point of view... We live on this earth right now for a reason beyond our comprehension, beyond this dimension. What we create here has an impact that we cannot conceive.

So, what if taking care of your clothes was a given way of expanding your contribution to this planet? What if it becomes part of the support system of you making a greater impact in this world and achieving deeper connections? I'll let you dig deeper into that!

Q. I feel clothes are such a lavish way to pamper myself. What do I do?

A. What if the first question here was: how abundant do I feel in these clothes?

Remember, we're energy, the Universe only understands energy.

What if this "lavish abundance" was in fact where you've belonged all along and these clothes are a way for you to anchor that frequency on days when you go back to these self-limiting beliefs?

Y - The Yes-er

My beautiful Y, you're the person who identifies as the "easygoing one". You say yes to everything!

I believe your approach in life can be a great one – *say yes to life!* – but only if you put yourself first and create the right boundaries to honour *yourself*! That way saying yes to life could mean living fully, welcoming all the goodness that comes in your way, including beautiful pieces to add in your closet.

But you must be careful you don't forget the first step: always checking in with yourself first.
You're always there for your family and friends with your selfless nature; more often than not, you tend to forget to be there for yourself.

Keep this in mind, we always need to put on our oxygen mask first, before helping others put on theirs. If you suffocate, you can't and won't be there to complete your mission.

So, tell me Y, are boundaries a thing for you?

THE YES-ER STYLE PROFILE

You have the down-to-earth next-door neighbour type vibe. You're very approachable, and your clothes normally demonstrate that effortlessness.

That's why you don't naturally consider spending money on clothes; you tend to value convenience.

WHAT KEEPS THE YES-ER STUCK AND FUNKED?

Being the one who always says yes, you probably find yourself at home dealing with the consequences.

While that open and positive energy is something we can all learn from you, it can have a shadow to it, which may be why you feel disconnected from your closet.

You say yes to all the external things, but the question here: are you saying no to yourself when you do that? Your wardrobe is a reflection of that answer.

If you're a pure Yes-er, your wardrobe may be packed with clothes that are far from connected to your essence, but you said yes to them because:

- Your mum/sister/friend was getting rid of that "like new" sweater/skirt/pair of pants/shoes, and you said, "Oh, what a waste! I'll keep it!"
- They were on sale, such an awesome deal! You had no idea how to pair it with anything in your closet, but you just couldn't say no to that kind of deal.
- Even though it wasn't your size, it was a total bargain, and you were going to lose/gain weight anyway.
- It was such good value and quality at the thrift store, you couldn't leave that item there.

Notice how there's not a single sign of honouring your soul in that list, but only your commitment to saying yes.

It's all about external circumstances and the complete avoidance of checking in with yourself if that piece is connected to you in any way.

THE YES-ER S.T.Y.L.E. IDENTITY SHIFT

Oh my dear Y, can you maybe put yourself in the equation? Here are a few clues how:

Clue #1:
GET QUIET, ALLOW SPACE, LET THINGS FLOW

Sit in front of your closet. What do you really want to see in front of you? How do you want to feel when you see it?

Journal all those thoughts. Writing down your feelings will be key for you to step into that highest version of yourself.

Allow the pieces to flow, just like your beautiful energy, and start asking the Universe for what *you* want so that you can connect to the ideal version of yourself.

What's *your* ideal style? Forget about circumstances. Look at it this way. There's lots of people out there who *are* connected to the pieces you're keeping in your closet, the pieces that aren't honouring you. You could be lighting up somebody else's life by releasing those clothes.

Clue #2:
OPEN YOUR ENERGY

Reflect on this style shift question and listen to what comes through:

What would it look like for me to honour myself first?

Pop that question to the Universe a few times a day and see what you experience.

Don't stop on the *how*, just ask *what* and let the Universe take care of the rest. Give yourself the luxury of asking for *yourself*.

One #3:
ADD THIS PATTERN INTERRUPT

Next time, before saying yes to adding more stuff* into your wardrobe, ask yourself, "Is this aligned with my ultimate wardrobe vision?"

Stuff meaning clothes that are supposed to light up somebody else but are just not you, so they're taking space in your closet, shifting the energy of your wardrobe in the wrong direction.

Instead of having a closet that could be filled with pieces that truly, whole-heartedly connect with you and being excited to wear them, if you keep saying yes to every piece, you can imagine where you'll be a year from now.

Purging your old stuff will be a big part of your process. Before you buy any more pieces, stand in your power and be brave enough to throw away clothes that you know aren't meant to be in your closet.

Convenient, cheap and *what a waste!* are words that you might want to be aware of when talking about your clothes.

Before you go shopping for anything new, and even before your ultimate decluttering session, arm yourself with all the Style Power tools in the coming chapters.

It's time to put yourself first. If you don't, it will send a sign to the Universe about how you're meant to be treated and give permission to those around you to do the same. You can do this!

YES-ER Q&A

Q. Where do I even start getting rid of stuff?
A. We'll get there. For now, become aware of this pattern and focus on interrupting it. Recognise that saying no doesn't mean you're not honouring yourself. In fact, saying no might help you take your expansion to the next level.

Q. Does this mean I need to change my identity?
A. Absolutely not! This is an exercise for you to become aware of how getting too caught up on saying yes might have taken you to a place of stagnation. You might want to shift your identity at some point in your life, and you might not. This classification is here to bring awareness to you and help you up-level your wardrobe. The whole idea is for you to keep letting the river flow and letting your energy flow the same way.

*

L - The Lawbreaker

My dear L, I love how enthusiastically you love to break the rules. You might even proclaim it proudly.

The rebel inside of you just wants to break free and forge your own path.

You're about creating your own version of everything, and that's a powerful skill.

You're a revolutionary. In everything you do, you ignite the fire inside, and it's so beautiful to see.

You won't take no for an answer. You always try to look for

unconventional ways to go about things. You aren't okay following rules for the sake of it.

THE LAWBREAKER STYLE PROFILE

Your wardrobe is definitely no exception to that rebelliousness. You love to break standards, push limits and create a statement.

You want to express your unwavering unique point of view in life, including with your clothes.

You have an innate desire to show who you are. You do it in every aspect of your life, and your clothes are the first to be invited to the party.

WHAT KEEPS THE LAWBREAKER STUCK AND FUNKED?

Stephen Covey refers to this concept in his book *The 7 Habits of Highly Effective People*. When wanting to stand apart from something becomes the centre of your life, you end up conditioning your whole existence upon it. That's the antithesis of freedom.

The only caveat that can keep you stuck and wondering why you don't find yourself in the mirror anymore is that you might have focused *too much* on breaking rules. So much so that you've forgotten the most important goal of creating your outfits to highlight *you*, your ultimate essence, which in turn sets you *free*.

There's a difference between making you the main character of your style inspiration and putting your ideology at the centre of your style.

That might be why things aren't working and maybe why you felt attracted to this book, which is all about escaping the rules and creating harmony with your true nature on our own terms.

Because of your innate drive to carve your own path, you can get side-tracked and unconsciously follow a rule – one of rebelling at all costs – that'll take you further from your true light.

In other words, wanting to stay away from the general rules, you might end up following another anti-rule. And if you're not taking aesthetics into account, opposing all the style rules can lead to a style disaster.

It's all about finding *balance*.

I know this sounds hilarious to you, but I highly encourage you to pay attention, as balance in style might break some of your preconceptions.

Without knowing some basic design guidance, you might end up feeling a mess and unable to find yourself when you look in the mirror.

And that right there might be the reason why you feel stuck in your style.

THE LAWBREAKER S.T.Y.L.E. IDENTITY SHIFT

Here are some clues as to where you might start. Not rules, just clues!

One #1:
MEDITATING JUST FOR THE SAKE OF BEING

Focus your meditation on:

I am

Sit with the reality that you just *are*, and you don't need to stand out from everyone else because you already are unique. We're here to honour that essence of you. We don't need to try to differentiate you, as it's already there. We're simply going to make it shine even brighter with the support system that best works for you.

One #2:
OPEN YOUR ENERGY

Reflect on this style shift question as a way of opening your energy to what could be out there for you.

What would it look like to see me first?

Sit with this question, repeat it a few times a day and see what comes up.

If you've lost track of your inner-outer alignment and ended up with a closet that's not honouring you but only reflects your law-breaking tendencies, it might be time to turn around that outward-looking mirror and start listening to what you feel inside.

One #3:
STAND OUT FROM THE CROWD

Stand apart (or ahead) of the masses by finding out more about your colours. (We'll expand on this in Chapter 6).

Learn about your personal palette and how much of you you can find in it.

Then have a good time bringing your personality into your appearance and seeing the harmonious trailblazer within you when you stand in front of the mirror every morning.

Once you have that knowledge in your pocket, bend all the rules in this book if you like and have fun making your style yours with your divine and magnificent ability to express yourself.

LAWBREAKER Q&A

Q. I love my identity and what I stand for. Is this misaligned with creating a style that stands apart from the masses?

A. Here's the thing. You don't need to try to stand apart. It's already your identity. It's a matter of understanding how this game of style works and then, from that position of power, moving your pieces. It's not about one or the other. We can converge it all for your ultimate benefit.

Q. What does this identity awareness tell me about what my style is missing?

A. That you're a trailblazer, and when you honour that, you won't ever stop up-levelling your style game. What you learn in this book will stay with you forever.

*

E - The Early Adopter

My beautiful E, you're a trend follower, no matter what. You love browsing fashion magazines and staying up-to-date with seasonal trends. Some people might call you a fashion victim, and you laugh admitting it.

Those two words? I never use them. I believe being a victim in *any* scenario isn't a position where you're *owning* your infinite potential. Instead, I'd say you're a fashion lover. (Words are power. Never forget that!).

A love for fashion, and that's the truth. Fashion is one of your confessed addictions. You love admiring and following new trends. You don't like waiting for the sales to start. (You literally can't help it).

Your love for fashion means you can fall into wearing outfits that are completely disconnected to who you are on the inside, and you wonder *why* so many times.

You may also tend to end up with too much clutter that ultimately won't fit with your desire to evolve.

EARLY ADOPTER STYLE PROFILE
You look put-together and take your style seriously.

Looking good is a high value of yours, and following the latest trends gives you a sensation of being on top of your style game; and in a way, on top of life.

You have a fearless approach when it comes to staying ahead of the curve. You take pride in being innovative.

And ideally, you'd like to feel this way in everything you do.

WHAT KEEPS AN EARLY ADOPTER STUCK AND FUNKED?
If you're feeling stuck and in a funk about your wardrobe, let me share with you a quote that I have hanging in my office:

Fashion is what you buy. Style is what you do with it.
- Unknown

You might have reached a point where you look yourself in the mirror and, most of the time, don't see or connect with yourself.

And that's completely normal as you might have lost touch with yourself in these busy days, focusing too much on others' perception of style.

Your passion for fashion (my son Tom would point out how that rhymes) is admirable and something you're proud of, as you absolutely should be.

It's just a matter of shifting the inner disconnection that you feel has led you to get stuck.

In addition, the reason why you might not feel at peace with so much clutter is because your ultimate essence doesn't feel at peace with it. And that's okay too. It's a matter of understanding how to create a wardrobe that aligns with your ultimate nature; only adding pieces that honour you and contribute to your life and wardrobe.

EARLY ADOPTER S.T.Y.L.E. IDENTITY SHIFT

Following trends doesn't have to be incompatible with listening to your heart and expressing your personality. Check out these clues for what to do next.

One #1:
WORK ON INCREASING YOUR BODY AWARENESS

The exercise I mention in Chapter 2 to increase your body-mind connection will be especially beneficial for you.

Sit with your eyes closed and become aware of how it feels to be inside your sacred temple. This will help you warm up your muscles by being in sync with your body and what it's asking for.

One #2:
OPEN YOUR ENERGY

Use this style shift question to open your energy:

What would it look like for me to feel in complete harmony with my body and what I wear?

Put it out there for the next few days and see what comes to you in reply.

One #3:
PAY SPECIAL ATTENTION

Be mindful of how you want to embed your personality into your everyday style. This is the perfect way to highlight your personality within all the new trends you choose to follow. Listen to what your body is asking for first.

EARLY ADOPTER Q&A

Q. Does this mean that following trends isn't aligned with my highest good?

A. Absolutely not. This is an exercise for you to introduce mindfulness into your style outlook, a call for you to listen to your body first, and understand that not all trends need to be followed by you for you to be ahead of the curve.

It might also mean that you keep following the same trends but reclaiming a whole lot of personal power too, which will result in a completely different outcome, showing up with 10 times the magnetism, 10 times the positive self-perception and 10 times the impact you'll make in the world.

It's one thing to stay current and a completely different thing to stay disconnected. My aim is to show you how you could picture being both and benefit more from your fashion passion.

Q. What if I love a trend that won't fit with what I discover about dressing my body?
A. Where there's a will, there's a way. We're not here to restrict your style. We're here to enhance it and expand it. The dressing your body chapters later on in this book are not here to limit you but to expand your wings.

EXPERIMENTING WITH YOUR S.T.Y.L.E. IDENTITY

As I said earlier, I created these identities inspired by the different approaches we all have to the common action of getting dressed and the meaning we all give to having a wardrobe full of clothes.

You can identify another trait in your identity and shift it with the tools in this book. It's all a matter of increasing your awareness so you can keep moving forward in this area, but also extrapolate it to all areas in your life.

How do you know if you need to change? Well, is the identity you hold keeping you from achieving your goals? What shift could you adopt to make your vision happen? It doesn't necessarily need to substitute the identity you have, but notice if the identity you're holding on to is helping you move forward towards your vision or keeping you stuck and "safe".

The point is how you show up in your closet might give you a hint of how you show up in your life and your business. Are you ready to bust those limitations? Let's keep moving forward.

Now that you know your sense of self, your vision and your identity, it's just a matter of focusing your attention on the rest of the Style Power Formula. Once you've got the tools to connect to yourself, recognise who you are, where you are and what body you're in, it'll make things easier for you to go through the rest of the Style Power Formula and finally be able to reconnect with yourself in the mirror.

We're cosmic beings having a human experience. Acknowledge where you are in your human experience. It is magically and constantly evolving. Then start showing up in the world as you want to be.

Before you go any further, you might want to revisit your vision now that you know more about the identities that keep you stuck. Do you need to make your vision even bigger?

Summary of S.T.Y.L.E. identities

IDENTITY	STYLE PROFILE
S SAFE PLAYER	Plays it safe, loves predictability and being appropriate.
T TUNED-IN	Intuitive, highly self-aware, dresses how they feel.
Y YES-ER	Easygoing, adaptable and accommodating to others.
L LAWBREAKER	Loves going against the norm and standing out.
E EARLY ADOPTER	Loves new trends and feeling ahead of the curve.

STUCK	SHIFT QUESTION
Has lost connection to what they really want. Feels lost when it comes to innovation.	What would it look like for me to express myself through clothes feeling safe? Spend 10 days in a row sitting in silence and going within for 20 minutes. Use inner connection tools (Chapter 1).
Has lost touch with the outside and the visual game of style.	What would it look like to create a style that reflects me in 3D with ease and joy? Pay special attention to the visual style tools in Chapter 8. They'll take your intuitive style to the next level, giving it shape in 3D.
Has ended up with a cluttered closet full of pieces that don't reflect them as a person.	What would it look like for me to honour myself first? Identify very accurately your personality in style (Chapter 7). This will be key for you to nail the Style Power Formula as well as to say no to what doesn't do it for you.
Has lost track of creating inner-outer alignment ending up with a closet that's not honouring them.	What would it look like to be me first? Meditate on this and increase your personal awareness identifying your colour palette. Enjoy bending the (un)conventional style rules to honour your revolutionary nature.
Has a hard time connecting energetically with their wardrobe.	What would it look like for me to feel in complete harmony with my body and what I wear? Pay special attention to your Personality Style that'll show you the way to that connection.

CHAPTER FIVE

Saying no to the style status quo *

HAVE FUN AND LET GO AGAIN

The most important aspect when it comes to choosing your clothes is that you feel at ease. When I first finished my image consultant training, I was overwhelmed for a long time, and that meant I was overwhelming my clients too because there were so many rules I wanted to follow. I had this need to be perfect, but I now see I was missing the point!

The beauty of style is in having fun, playing, bending the rules. That's where I felt and will always feel alive. That's why self-exploration and self-discovery are key for you to master dressing yourself.

Because only *you* know yourself the way you do, and having that "inside scoop" will help you identify what version of style makes you feel alive.

Let's say mainstream style rules tell us we shouldn't wear pleats if we have volume or curves. I say if your personality wants to take you there, just *find* the way!

Let go of perfection. Let go of looking just like that catalogue photo or wearing that exact garment the way it's worn by somebody else. Let go of having to always look thinner or taller or wider or...

When you let go and start having fun, your joy and eagerness to show up for yourself will mean that you find the type of pleats that work for you, your shape and your personality. Maybe, for instance, that's custom-made. It might be that same skirt with a tight jacket that defines your waist. It might be the same type of pants with a pleated front made of a heavier fabric, so they don't create so much volume. The possibilities are endless!

The most important part is that you feel *free* and legitimately eligible to wear the fashion you *want* to wear. Once you work from the Style Power Formula, this will be so much easier, and it will work for you.

Read that again. **It *will* work.**

Even if we're talking about wearing a plain white t-shirt on stage, the state or energy or *attitude* that you use to choose and wear that t-shirt will make all the difference!

Remember, all I'm sharing is simple and intuitive. This is how I do it. And it works.

PEARLS AND PEYTO LAKE

Did you know that an oyster is created as a reaction between the mollusc to an intruder; that pearls are created as a consequence of a set of accidental conditions? I love pearls. They embody elegance, class, old money, beauty and miracles, all at once.

I have a picture in my office of Peyto Lake from our honeymoon in the Rocky Mountains. I always felt connected to that place and its magnificent turquoise colour that looks almost photoshopped. When I printed the photo onto a canvas for my office, I googled more about it.

Apparently, the colour of the lake is created by the glacier crystals that fall from the mountain. When the light reflects those crystals, we perceive that stunning bright turquoise colour. In the end, it's *just a lake*, but that magic dust falling from above makes it so unique.

Your style is just like pearls and Peyto Lake.

On the outside, it's just about the clothes you buy, but when you allow that magic dust to fall from above, when you allow the oyster to create you a pearl, your whole style game takes on a different colour, and it will have the most marvellous look to it. Inevitably, magic is created.

After you do this work, when you see yourself in the mirror, you will connect to that inner child, the one you still have inside, who recognised themselves when they saw their image in the mirror. They may have become lost in external learning, but you can go back to dancing like nobody's watching.

I'm not saying that there won't be days when you won't like what you see, but the aim here is to love it anyway, no matter what, accept it and embrace it. You always have a choice between seeing yourself through the eyes of unconditional love and acceptance or seeing yourself with a critical eye.

There's a reason why each pearl has the shape it has. The many crystals that decided to embed in a certain way form that unique miracle. And there's a correspondence between how your body looks and what your personality is like. (I'll cover this some more in Chapter 7).

Just like with pearls and Peyto Lake, you're meant to shine in your own specific way. It's no accident that you are the way you are.

RED LIPSTICK

"Pay attention to what I have to say!"
This is why I'm such a big fan of red lipstick.

It's said to be equivalent to ties in men. It infuses women with this non-verbal message. I believe men and women are equal. And equal means equal. I don't believe in making women more than men as a punishment for all we've suffered throughout history, and at the same time, I believe our boundaries to protect our power as women need to be stronger than ever.

I'm a mother of two ah-mazing boys, who one day will become adults and who I really hope (at least I'm doing my best) will hold women in the highest regard.

I wear red lipstick because I feel eligible to wear "my tie" whenever I please. Some days, you just need to demand a little extra authority; others, you wear it to feel more feminine.

The one thing I tell women is to make sure it's the right shade of red as there's a big difference between a warm and a cool red (more on this in Chapter 6).

My friend Laura in Spain told me an interesting story about her experience of wearing red lipstick in the workplace. It made me reflect once again on how much work we still need to do as a community to eliminate stigmas around women and power.

Laura was having issues with another workmate, who incidentally was another woman. Apparently, this workmate felt threatened by my friend, or so she was told by a freelance coach hired by the company, who also happened to be a woman.

After talking to all the employees, this coach decided to smooth things out by asking Laura to stop wearing red lipstick as that was being interpreted as a threat by the workmate in question.

The reason? Some women feel threatened by other women when they stand their ground and show up *owning* their personal power. And wearing red lipstick is *all* about owning your personal power.

I believe we have a responsibility to stop this toxic stigma. Women are so powerful. We don't see men asking other men to remove their tie because it's acting as a threat to their workmates.

Our personal power isn't a limited resource. Just because another person shines their light, there's no less supply for us.

So long as any woman is not allowed to be who she is and reinforced to stay in her victim mentality, feeling overpowered by other women, we won't move forward as women.

Starting from right now, I ask you, my dear reader, whoever you are, whatever your gender, would you help me support women to stand their ground? This is the very reason I started this book with self-discovery and designing what 'our ground' looks like. When you live from a place of connection, you'll be the one *building* bridges and supplying the lipstick!

We aren't two, or three, or even 1,000 teams… We are one. One team that made it possible for you to be here. One team that creates societies the world over. We won't move in the right direction until we embrace our sacred and diverse unity.

As for Laura, the day after she was told to discontinue wearing red lipstick, all the other women in her office besides the one who had felt threatened wore red lipstick along with my friend. Was this an attempt to get revenge? I want to believe not. I see it as an attempt to normalise standing in their power together as women. This is the kind of support we can give to each other, and that's the kind of spirit that makes me proud to be a woman, proud to be a wife to an amazing man who cheers me up when I wear my sneakers and my red lipstick and when my kids may or may not have walked around half the day with red lipstick marks on their faces... I'm also amazingly proud of having male friends who I adore and support with all my heart just as much as my girlfriends.

Let's make the rest of this book on owning your style about building sacred bridges and togetherness: first and foremost with yourself, with your people, and with all of us as a big community.

We're all part of the whole. The more of us who acknowledge it, the more we'll thrive as a team.

THE #1 STYLE MYTH
"It's hard to look effortless."

I was right there believing this myth for my whole life until my early thirties. I tried so hard to nail "effortless style". Well, can we just call it quits on trying so hard to be *effortless*? Oh, the irony! I was totally missing the point.

The problem? I was too focused on pleasing others and looking like others that I didn't stop for a second and realise I wasn't honouring myself.

Most importantly, I was missing the chance to see style as a way to connect with my body and the real version of me.

At uni, I had two fabulous friends. They were beautiful, and thinner and shorter than me, so my tall girl syndrome from my school years was repeating itself.

I starved myself, mainly eating salads to stay thin and working out like a maniac. I wore clothes that would fit but wouldn't make me look *fat*. Clothes were so important that I'd even plan my party outfits for each weekend at the beginning of the month!

It was all about trying to match my friends' beauty standards. It was all about looking outside instead of inside.

Okay, so I had become a bit better than I was in high school, where I only wore my classic outfit of polo shirt/sweater, coloured jeans (usually from Zara), and nautical shoes.

Nowadays, I look at those garments and cringe because I still love a shirt, but definitely not the shapeless ones I used to wear back then – my womanly figure in girls' clothes. Girls' clothes were too small for me, and I needed to wear women's clothes at a young age, but I felt ashamed of it. I didn't even wear a proper bra until I was 16 or 17, as I was too embarrassed to show any signs of growing up "too fast".

Having spent too long trying to hide who I was, it became the norm, so when it came to growing up and finding my voice, I was lost there too. Having a family who always loved me and being spoiled as the youngest of three sisters (with my sisters being 14 and 17 years older than me), I always felt safe and protected, but in my early twenties, I reached the point of needing to find myself. And oh boy, was that a journey!

That's why I always encourage my little boys to choose, to listen to what they want, and always believe they're their own best friend. As much as I have awareness as their mum, we can only do the best for our current awareness, but they know themselves the best. That way, they'll be able to lay the foundations of true, healthy relationships with their friends and family. That combined with giving them as much love as I received and making sure they feel it.

The point of all this is to let you know that if I was able to identify my personality in the way I dress, you can too! (More on this coming up in Chapter 7).

COLOUR? WHAT COLOUR?

The day I discovered the difference between wearing energetically aligned shades and wearing any other colour, I felt sad, disappointed, even depressed. You might have thought it was a breakthrough, but it was the day I realised that I'd spent a whole lot of money on "revolutionary image consulting training", training that I had been wanting to do for so many years, only to discover that I'd been avoiding myself this whole time.

The colours that came out as being my "perfect palette" were nothing like the ones I'd wear or had in my closet. I didn't think those colours were cool or fashionable.

Now I realise that when that olive green drape approached my face, it wasn't the colour I was rejecting; I just didn't like the fact that I could see myself in the mirror.

If we've been unconsciously trying to avoid ourselves by wearing colours that disguise us, how on earth are we going to identify consciously what's really going on inside of us?

At age 12, my parents decided that it would be best for me to move from a very modern-minded, new-money (as it was called at the time) private school where I was called by my first name and was feeling on top of things to the complete antithesis – a very traditional, conservative, serious, old city, historic school where I was called by my last name.

That transition was hard to say the least. I still remember the first day in the new school as if it was yesterday. How embarrassed I felt when the teacher, who for some reason didn't seem to like me, asked me:

"Are you repeating classes, Barrero?"

It was the first question he asked, and my world caved in.

How could he not see just by looking at me how excellent I was? (*Duh!*) Little did I know how the world really worked. I wasn't going to be wrapped in cotton wool or treated with encouragement around here. That's not real life.

I went from having a teacher who was my confidante and offered to hide my tampons and pads in her personal cupboard (because at the age of 11, I was a girl who had her period way before anybody else I knew – Miss Catalina, what a great woman she was) to this patriarchal, conservative cold system full of male teachers who wouldn't even think about the idea of f e e l i n g s.

So yes, I abruptly came across the real world at age 12. Only now do I understand that this happened *for* me and not *to* me. Back then, all I knew was things hadn't started out right because that very first question assumed I was a failure only because I was judged by my appearance (ouch!). That's how I, as a "good girl" who always followed the rules, interpreted the question about whether I was repeating a year.

What I wasn't expecting was that my classmates would also call me by my last name, but only the boys. So it was that I learned to create that distance from myself; that apparently was how girls stayed happy in that school.

Needless to say, the most formative years of my life – ages 12 to 18 – were quite challenging. Surprised much? I felt the most inappropriate girl of all, always trying to hide the fact that I was taller (to be more specific, one head taller than the whole class except one boy), bigger and louder than anybody else, always trying to hide my witty personality. The fear of being judged far outweighed any intention to speak up.

Fast forward to that colour consultation in Canada, where I had been able to free myself and learn my calling because I had come face-to-face with the reality that I didn't like to see myself in the mirror, and that would have to change.

I've come so far from where I was 12 years ago when I had my colours done for the first time.

What makes colour my favourite transformational tool when it comes to experimenting with your wardrobe and appearance?

Its energetic power of helping you connect with yourself of uplifting your spirits on cloudy days, metaphorically and literally.

And so, it seems natural for us to get into the (Un)conventional Style Tools part of the Style Power Formula.

I hope by now you have seen that fun and play and an openness to experiment are going to be key to the next phase of your journey. You have explored your inner self and your style identity. Now it's time to meet the (Un)conventional Style Tools that complete the Style Power Formula. Let's see first how colour and personality combine to help you dress on the outside as you feel on the inside.

The next chapters will be all about discovering the wardrobe, image, appearance, style and clothing tools that helped me uncover the thin (or thick) veil that once was standing between who I was on the inside and what I could be on the outside.

Am I done yet? Not even close! In fact, now that I know these tricks, the ways I show up get better and better with age. They will never end. They will keep evolving. And that's the beauty of the Style Power Formula. It keeps on giving.

PILLAR THREE

(Un)Conventional Style Tools

NOBODY KNOWS YOUR BODY BETTER THAN YOU.
OWN IT AND ALLOW IT.

Let's dig into the third and final pillar of the Style Power
Formula where we'll be working from the outside-in.

The (Un)conventional Style Tools include:
Colour Magic
Personality in Style
The Visual Game

The main goal of this third pillar is for you to understand
how you can dress yourself, always honouring the real
and authentic you. We're here to show the world that
uniqueness of yours from the inside out, and these (Un)
conventional Style Tools will help you materialise (show
in 3D) all the work you have done in this book until now.

All these tools are included for you to create a style that
harmonises completely with who you truly are. With these
tools, you can show up unapologetically as 100% you,
standing tall and proud of showing the world the unique
person that you are in this reality.

By doing this, you're aligning to your ultimate work in
this lifetime, honouring the unique genetic coding that
makes you an indispensable part of this world. With these
tools, shining your light will be a given in your life from
now on.

CHAPTER SIX

Colour Magic *

A DIFFERENT KIND OF COLOUR ANALYSIS

The most important aspect of it all, colour has an *instant* energetic effect on you. Take it from a recovered black and grey wearer, this tool changed my life.

The one thing that colour will require from you is commitment, but it's a fun one if you choose to stick *reasonably* close to your palette and then, after a few weeks, see how you feel about wearing old colours again.

Let me give you a word of warning. It might be the case that your personality and colouring might seem to clash. I totally get it! But I promise there's always a way around this so that you can bring out your personality.

The most important part is to not only see the effects that colour has on your appearance but also develop a sensitivity for how your energy shifts with different colouring. Why? Because in most cases, the outer effects don't seem to be powerful enough to convince people to make a commitment to sticking to their colours. I've found that the visual effect of colour is not enough on its own to get people to do this work. (It's like losing weight to look good for other people. Never works! Only by having a personal reason will the weight stay off. Same with sticking to your colours. The reason for doing this has to be from within.) The real shift in your behaviour comes when you focus on developing an awareness of how your body feels as well as the outstanding effect on your appearance.

From what you wear to what surrounds you to what you use every day, colour is in everything. And when it comes to clothes, it's 90% about how you *feel* when you see yourself in the mirror once you start living inside the world of your magical palette.

If you have an artistic background, it might be easier for you to tell the difference between a whole variety of shades. If you don't have any artistic background whatsoever, like me as an ex-financial auditor, don't feel discouraged if colour doesn't click immediately because we can also do it 100%.

I get it, though. If you're anything like me, you might be tired of those magazine colour palette tests because I could never tell the difference between pink and orange blush at first, and that's what it was telling me.

Here, you're in for a very different kind of "colour analysis". In this book, you're going to identify colours that *honour* you, not just "look good" on you. These colours will make you feel alive and seen.

And most importantly, I've made sure to give you all the systems, so you can finally identify the uniqueness of your body – to me, the most important part.

DRESSING IN THE COLOUR YOU FEEL

Every morning I wake up and connect in meditation with my body. I ask my cells what colour we want to be infused with today. Every time, it's a different colour. And that's the colour inspiration I choose to take with me and wear that day.

Now, this might not mean dressing head to toe in that colour. It could be the colour of your underwear or just one piece of clothing, but whatever you choose, that inner-outer connection feels rejuvenating and expansive.

Amazingly, 99% of the time, the colour *will* be within my palette, as I feel so connected to those colours that's what feels natural. This is what happens with colour. Once you go through this deeply expansive colour magic process, you'll be able to see, if you're willing, and feel the difference certain colours make to your whole system at an emotional, physical and energetic level.

The more awareness my clients have and are open to having, the easier this process becomes, no matter what their artistic background has been. Due to the energetic nature of this process, you'll find that you will become more and more aware of the difference certain colours make when wearing them.

It'll become more and more obvious on the outside too, as I find the effects are more noticeable as we age, due to the fact that our magic palette helps us create a flawless harmony with our natural features and our colours create less shade that shows up wrinkles and face "imperfections". Instead, those features become part of that beautiful harmony of yours too.

THE DIFFERENCE BETWEEN WEARING THE COLOUR OR THE COLOUR WEARING YOU

I'm sure you can recall a time when you wore a colour or certain colours and people gave you compliments on how gorgeous that colour looked on you. Sometimes they'll say it that way. Other times they might say, "What a beautiful colour you're wearing."

Here's the difference:
When you're wearing a colour that suits you and your energy, the eye will

automatically travel to your face, highlighting your best features, hence why people would say how great a certain colour looks on *you*. When the colour isn't harmonising with your natural colouring, the colour will *pop* first.

Our aim is to create a style that empowers you instead of dimming that light of yours. This is one more reason why I see colour as a *key* piece of this empowerment journey.

Style Power Practice

COLOUR MAGIC KICKSTART

So, let's kickstart the discovery of your colours. How will we do that? Well, first, by discarding 50% of the spectrum, for you to be able to see yourself and discover the attractive, open, honest, proud, unapologetic, whole version of yourself.

By seeing how your "better half" of the colour spectrum makes you feel and the effects it has on your face, you might be encouraged to keep digging until you find the *ultimate* palette or this information might be enough for you to take action. Either way, just by identifying what the "better half" of the colour spectrum looks like for you, your wardrobe life can radically change for the better.

The palettes

To support this section, I've created a resource for you at **www.stylepowerbook.com**

All the palettes you're going to discover in this process are my images of physical palettes created by my dear friend and mentor Karen Brunger, from the International Image Institute.

The reason I've always used only these and not others is because there's an energetic reason for those colours to be in each palette; in other words, all the colours in your palette are perfectly chosen and have the same energy in common, an energy that's aligned with you. A new energy will also be created *between* you and the palette.

The process

All the tools you need are in the resource content at **www.stylepowerbook.com**

Step #1
PREPARATION

The first step to discovering your colour palette is to take a picture of yourself in natural light, ideally at midday when the light is at its best.

If you wear makeup, it's best to remove it, as well as any jewellery, glasses and/or coloured contact lenses.

If your hair is dyed, it's best to keep it out of the picture when you go through the process by cropping it. If your hair is not dyed, your natural hair colour will help a lot in the process, so leave it in.

For men, having some facial hair will help.

Follow the instructions on how to crop your photo in the bonus tool I created for you.

Step #2
WARM OR COOL?

With this process, you're going to be able to determine whether your ideal magic palette leans more towards cooler colours or warmer ones. Your skin pigments determine your particular skin colour, which is why your colouring doesn't change after going through puberty.

The three skin pigments are:

- haemoglobin
- melanin
- carotene

The specific combination of these three will give you the key to understanding how certain colours blend with your skin colour, while others just won't.

When talking about warm and cool, it has nothing to do with "how cool" you are. (You and I both know you're the coolest cause you're reading this book!)

We're talking about your undertone, which means discovering how your skin tends to have a blue or yellow tone underlying it, which is very well perceived when bringing different shades next to it.

Now it might be the case you find yourself in the middle of

two palettes. I find 99.9% of the time, you'll always find one that'll look slightly better. Instead of getting stuck or creating self-judgement when that happens, acknowledge that it might be a sign that your colouring is more neutral, and that's why it might be more challenging to see at the beginning.

Step #3
HOW DO WE KNOW?

Once you add your picture to the cool and warm palette slides in the resources section, it's time to flip back and forward both slides and understand what it is that you're looking for.

What to look at to understand if a certain palette suits you or not:

- **Your natural lip colour:** With the most accurate palette, you'll find the colour of your lips will intensify.
- **Your teeth:** Teeth will look whiter with the palette that suits you best.
- **Undereye:** Dark circles under your eyes will intensify with the least appealing palette.
- **Your eyes:** The whites of your eyes will also look whiter with the better palette.
- **Your jaw:** Your jaw will uplift with the more accurate palette, whereas with the one that doesn't sit well with you, your jaw will visually drop.
- **Wrinkles and expression marks:** When wearing the most accurate palette, these sorts of marks will be less noticeable because the better palette tends to reduce the shadow on your face.

- **Skin colour:** Skin will look healthiest in your colour palette. Not yellowish, not blue, just healthier.
- **Eye colour:** Your eyes will look brighter, but this doesn't mean that blue eye colour will pop in the same way with all blues! (That applies to all eye colours). Depending on your undertone, it will be a warmer blue or a cooler blue.
- **Focus:** When putting your palette close to your face, you'll see harmony. The eye will travel naturally to your face. In the opposite case, the eye will travel first to the colour, and your head will look like it's flying on top of the colour instead of belonging to it.
- **Expressions:** Have a sense of where your facial expressions look more relaxed.

It's important that you compare both palettes *many* times, switching back and forward until you finally see it. If it gets to a point where you can't see the difference, distance yourself from it and come back later. Try not to get too much in your head. It's a Visual Game, but it's also an energetic one, remember.

Once you find yourself with the palette that "belongs" to you – either cool or warm – then you'll be able to explore further from there if you want.

I've created a free resource to help you go through this process. Go to **www.stylepowerbook.com** to find out what your "better half" is, where you'll have access to the palettes and colour experiments that can help you have more certainty.

This process will help you understand what your undertone is, which will allow you to eliminate 50% of the colours in the full spectrum. From there, you can choose to refine the process and find your ultimate palette with some professional feedback.

The reason I mention professional feedback is that, in order to refine and find the ultimate magic palette for you, you'll need some guidance to understand the language in which colour communicates with you. You can choose any pro you like. Just make sure they know about colour and energy and use palettes similar to the ones I'm showing to you, as that'll be key for you to notice that energetic shift.

Of course, you're more than welcome to request it from us, but above all, I wish for you to experience the magic.

COLOUR Q&A

Q. Is this my magic palette?

A. This process will help you discard 50% of the colours in the colour spectrum. Your magic palette will be a more precise version of it, and for that, you'll need expert feedback. However, just by knowing if you're cool or warm, you can start having a great sense of how colours can make a difference in your energetic field. Finding out your unique magic palette will be something you can always choose after.

Q. Will this result change if I'm tanned or have jaundice?

A. No, it won't change. No matter what you've heard in the past, trust me. After you've gone through puberty, your colours won't change.

Q. Is it okay if I wear other colours and then I wear my colours next to my face?

A. You might already know why I don't feel aligned with this! To me, the purpose of colour is to support us energetically. Does that mean I always wear my magic palette? Well, 90% of the time, I do! However, that's *not* because my goal is to look good or that I'm that perfectionist. Definitely not. (At least not in this case!) The only reason I practice this is because of how I feel in my colours. Now I feel naturally drawn to warm colours. They might not be *exactly* like the ones you see in my magic palette, but definitely close enough.

And this is a step-by-step process. It's not something you develop overnight. At the time I'm writing this work, I've been practising this art for 11 years. No, you don't have to spend so long nailing this; I have clients who, after a month working together, were even correcting me!

Q. What if I feel restricted having to wear only those colours?

A. Well, firstly, here's where I remind you that you don't *have* to. I'm showing you what works for me and for my clients who have followed this process religiously. There's a magic energy behind realising the effect certain colours have on you.

Also, remember that your palette is made of millions of colours. When you become aware of that magical shift in perception around colour, you'll be able to tell on the spot in a store if a colour honours you or doesn't. It is really that simple or not, depending on how you want to label it.

One of my clients, Julia, is a vegetarian and told me how she experienced the change of perspective on limiting her colours to one half of the spectrum.

"It's like being vegetarian. You don't have to look at the rest of the menu. You

just focus on the veggie area and enjoy your meal. It's only restrictive if you want to see it that way. To me, it's liberating, because I know what colours are going to work! I know that 90% of the colours in my palette match."

And that, my friend, is gold! I'll leave it up to you, but I do want to honour and acknowledge that it's a big leap of faith. And remember, you don't have to do it all at once. Just start little by little and see the difference it makes in your life.

Q. Why do I have so much resistance going for it?

A. That's okay. Progress not perfection, remember! We're here to find style tools that help us connect and honour ourselves in the most natural way. You can always come back to this part, but the energetic effect of this practice will be the one factor that'll make this work like magic. For that, you need to *believe*.

STYLE POWER

CHAPTER SEVEN

Personality in your style*

It's quiz time! (Yes, again!) This is the most effective, intuitive and fun method I've ever used for my clients to be able to express themselves in their style.

It's different to the S.T.Y.L.E. Identity because instead of talking about your natural habits when it comes to the relationship with your wardrobe, it helps you figure out your style personality.

What if I tell you I have a magic trick for you to start connecting to that innate sense of "knowing what to wear" right now and then taking it to the next level?

There's a direct expression on the outside of how you are on the inside. When you dress to enhance it, you own even more of your personal style. It's like wearing a badge of honour, standing proud in who you are and how you are.

There are very defined and sometimes extreme descriptions in these profiles. Rest assured, 90% of people are a combination of two or three of them. You might even find you're a mix of all of them, and that's completely okay.

The importance of shifting your awareness in this aspect is for you to keep discovering yourself and find the answer to the question:

What's my personal style?

Along the way, you'll probably realise that you now know a lot about what you love, what you don't like and what your personality when it comes to style might look like in this moment. While that might change, it's important to have a starting point and recognise how the different personalities magically show up as you evolve in your life.

For instance, more than 10 years ago, my Personality Styles were a mix of Elegant Sporty and Romantic.

Now, after being a mum and being so comfortable in casual outfits, I'd say I've developed more of a Natural and Creative side that I never thought I had, and I can 100% see that in my physical features. The Romantic side is still there, but it's not so developed these days. Elegant Sporty has always been my thing, but that doesn't mean that I don't dip my toe into my Romantic or Creative some days.

These archetypes are key for you to create anything in your life. It will help you to feel most in tune with your raw, authentic self. The days I have to create content in my business or tape videos, I make sure I'm always dressed in tune with my essence, so I can serve at my best.

As with everything you'll find in this book, there's no right or wrong. Explore your personality and have fun with it.

Fun fact: There's a real correlation between your Personality Style and your physique. That's the reason why I'm able to tap into your energy so quickly when I do one-to-ones and translate it into style. Some clients would think that I'm a psychic because I could tell their personality really fast. The truth is we all have our own signature essence. Energy never lies. In Canada, I worked with two clients who were identical twins; through this method, I was able to nail their personalities without even knowing them. Their way of talking, their gestures, even the way their identical features were defined gave me all the clues I needed to spot their Unique Personality Styles.

But most importantly, the way your energy shifts when you see yourself how you reflect your unique personality on the outside is that helps me to guide you to create a closet that 100% supports your evolution.

THE DOORWAY TO CONNECTING WITH YOUR FOUNDATION

The reason why I'm such a big fan of the Personality Styles is because this system will not only reflect you like your astrology chart but will help you find your foundation, your starting point in the external style game. These styles, far from limiting you to wearing a certain type of clothes, are meant to liberate you.

Defining your Personality Styles means you will be able to find your *planet aspects* in your *style chart* (I see you astro tribe) or understand why there are certain styles that make people say, "That's so you!"

As I said, these personalities can change throughout your lifetime, but they'll always take a different shape when worn by *you*.

No matter who my client is, I always give this example: The same type of garment will never look the same on two different people, not only because of the shape of that person but also because of the energy and style personality imprint that an individual has. Just like the same perfume smells different on every skin, your clothes will feel and project a different *fragrance* based on your natural essence.

For women, take this example:

A black, tight, tube, leather skirt.

Picture it on a woman with a straighter body shape, someone like Amal Clooney or Duchess of Sussex Megan Markle. That skirt will project feminine power with a strongly yang-predominant energy.

If you put that same skirt on Marilyn Monroe or Oprah Winfrey, the whole personality of that skirt changes. And the way that person feels in it changes too. That skirt will project messages of seduction, femininity and power, but coming from a yin-predominant energy.

Your Personality Style will 100% change the way you wear your clothes. Even if you try to replicate other people's styles, it will never look exactly the same because you're the main factor in the equation.

For men, here's another example:

A leather blazer.

Now, you might cringe when thinking about it or you might love it, depending on your personality, but stay with me for this one.

Picture the late James Dean in a leather blazer, and you're like, *Duh!* That guy rocks that jacket in the most exciting way, right?

Okay, now let's picture the same jacket on the late Sean Connery, certainly a lot different, agree? Connery projects a yang energy dominance that will infuse the jacket with authority.

That jacket will also send a very masculine message, but in a completely different way honouring a combination of yin and yang energy from a more authoritative place.

Giving you these examples helps you picture how understanding your own style personality archetype will be a powerful way to identify what's your personal twist on clothing and also why certain styles won't feel natural to you at the moment or maybe ever.

My style evolution has certainly shifted – from wearing high heels at university to living in sneakers as a mum – but my essence will always be there.

Don't get too caught up in the description of the upcoming archetypes, as they're deliberately exaggerated definitions of styles. However, do read them all and see what catches your eye.

Remember, this is all about honouring yourself. The style archetypes are simply a new filter to refine this tribute to your own unique light.

USING THE DUALITY OF BALANCE: YIN AND YANG

We are going to focus on the femaleness of the yin and the maleness of the yang duality to classify the Personality Style types. Keep in mind at all times that we are all a combination of both; just because you're a woman does not mean that your Personality Style will be yin-predominant and vice versa. I, for instance, have a lot of yang in my personality, and I'm very feminine. These aspects of the personalities are only to reflect the different roles that femaleness and maleness naturally represent in nature. We're not talking about gender here, but about duality and balance.

WHICH PERSONALITY STYLE IS YOURS?

Take this fun short test to get an idea of your Unique Personality Style. You might feel like choosing two or three of the options for one question. If that's the case, then do it! Go with your heart! Don't overthink it! Just remember it's all about you and your connection with your true self. There's no wrong answer if it's true to you.

Style Power Practice
PERSONALITY STYLE QUIZ

1. **When it comes to describing my body, what's my physical look?**
   A. Tall, slim and angular
   B. Average height to tall and strong build, medium to big bone structure
   C. Short to average height, compact and strong body
   D. Average height and body structure; very proportioned with no extremes
   E. Short height and delicate structure
   F. Voluptuous

2. **When it comes to my face, I have...**
   A. Angular features
   B. A broad or long facial shape and/or heavy eyebrows
   C. Eyes wide open and friendly perhaps a 'pixie' or boyish type of face
   D. Oval face with very proportioned features
   E. Soft and fine features – perhaps with pointy ears
   F. Rounded features, arched eyebrows and/or full lips

3. **I feel most attracted to...**
   A. Black
   B. Brown
   C. Green
   D. Pink
   E. Yellow
   F. Red

4. **My all-time dream profession involves...**
   A. Being CEO of a big company, top level executive, public relations
   B. Medicine, science or math
   C. Making the world a better place (social worker, author, professor, animal or nature related)
   D. Organisational skills, efficiency, process optimisation
   E. Being an artist, such as a poet, musician, designer, actor, dancer
   F. Being in the hospitality, beauty or massage industries

5. **In my professional life, I'm mostly driven by...**
   A. Wealth and prestige
   B. Achievement
   C. Ethics and/or ecology
   D. Organisation and order
   E. Self-expression
   F. Relationships

6. **I value...**
   A. Success, prestige, independence, exclusivity
   B. Education, athleticism, quality, good value, tradition
   C. Nature, authenticity, sustainability, human and animal rights, freedom

D. Good grooming, cleanliness, organisation, safety, control

E. Creativity, intuitiveness, mysticism, solitude

F. Family, friends, nurturing, pampering, service, luxury

7. My ideal style involves at least one of these words...

A. Fashion-forward, extreme, I like to be noticed

B. Tailored, comfortable, sporty and practical

C. Casual, comfortable, natural fabrics, eco-conscious

D. Coordinated, elegant, perfectly matching clothes

E. Unique, different, vintage, dreamy

F. Flowy, luxurious, elaborate, seductive

8. When I go shopping, I look for...

A. Exclusive pieces, expensive-looking, bold styles

B. Good quality, smart-casual clothes

C. Comfort, good price, breathable and natural materials

D. Jackets, skirts, classic pieces

E. Fun, unique pieces

F. Nice textures, beautiful details, pieces that hug my body

9. When it comes to accessories, I like...

A. Wearing one loud piece

B. Real jewellery (not custom) and a quality watch, not too much of it but high end

C. Not much, very simple if I wear anything, maybe wooden or woollen accessories

D. Always wearing jewellery, minimal and refined, especially pearls for women

E. Small and fine accessories, unique and different or vintage, also hats

F. Fancy and elaborated, a lot of details, also high-heel shoes

10. My dream house is...

   A. A penthouse in NYC by Central Park

   B. An old country estate or a castle

   C. A rustic and sustainable house close to the woods

   D. A traditional home in a good neighbourhood with white picket fence and a perfectly groomed lawn

   E. A warehouse in an artist district or any place with character

   F. Large luxurious home in a prestigious neighbourhood

11. My decorating style involves...

   A. Clean lines, minimum furniture, steel, glass, very modern

   B. Antiques, elegant style, large-scale pieces

   C. Very rustic style, predominantly brown and green colours, with a love of plants

   D. Classic, understated and elegant

   E. Unique, whimsical and creative

   F. Luxurious, with candelabras, mirrors, marble and glass finishes

12. If there were no limits, my favourite activity would be...

   A. Dining at first-class restaurants, partying, jet set lifestyle

   B. Horseback riding, walking the dogs, reading, board games, stimulating conversations

   C. Camping, being outdoors, looking for bargains, volunteering to make the world a better place

   D. Organising, keeping things clean, gardening, golf

   E. Daydreaming, meditating, writing, singing, designing, reading

   F. Cooking, having family and friends over, romantic dates, going to a spa

13. I come across as a...

    A. Striking, assertive and cool person

    B. Confident, educated and traditional person

    C. Casual, approachable and down-to-earth person

    D. Committed, accommodating and gracious person

    E. Joyful, expressive and fun person

    F. Caring, heartfelt, warm and sometimes flirtatious person

14. The type of shoe I would naturally choose is...

    A. Pointy and/or high-heeled shoe (like really high)

    B. Sturdy shoes, brogues and riding boots

    C. Birkenstock sandals, short boots, natural sneakers

    D. Classic pump, ballerinas, oxfords, moccasin

    E. Vintage boots, platform oxfords, coloured shoes, anything naturally different

    F. All of the beautiful shoes and more

Add up your score for each of the letters.
The archetype with the highest score is your style or style combo.

My Unique Personality Style looks

☐ A – Dramatic   ☐ D – Classic
☐ B – Elegant Sporty   ☐ E – Creative
☐ C – Natural   ☐ F – Romantic

Once you have your quiz result, keep going to find out what it all means.

YIN ENERGY PREDOMINANCE

ROMANTIC

Physical attributes

A typical Romantic is defined by curves, whether we're talking about facial features or silhouette. An artist wouldn't use straight lines when painting you.

Personality and style

You genuinely care about others. Your nurturing nature makes you the most typical model of a mother. You love taking care of all the family members and friends. Your dream work is always geared towards helping others and taking care of them.

You love extremely feminine styles, whether that's pink, flowery, soft styles or sexy, red bombshell styles; they both represent different sides of this style personality. You're pure feminine energy and may have a high level of sensuality as part of your energy.

You're naturally oriented towards beauty, and you love details and specific qualities. Textures are an important factor you take into account. Your senses are highly developed. You love indulging in yummy and luxurious food as well as nice-feeling fabrics, whether that might be for clothes or for your house.

You can't get enough accessories! That special sensitivity to touch is what motivates how much you enjoy soft fabrics that harmonise with your curvy features and body. You have a soft nature, and that's also your strength. By wearing soft fabrics and curved patterns, you highlight it!

What to look for

- For you, there aren't enough accessories. You're able to add many details to your outfit and still look fabulous. Pay attention to the shape of the accessories and details you choose: belt buckle, shoe point, earrings, pockets, tie knot, collars...
- Look for curvy styles that honour your natural body curves and try to stay away from stiff and linear fabrics.
- Pay attention to the patterns you use. You will usually look much more harmonious in rounded and curvy patterns rather than lines.
- Indulge in a style that makes you feel alive. You're all about your senses, so take this opportunity to dress in a way that honours your true nature: soft velvet, nice silks, lovely cashmere, high-quality organic cotton are all luxurious fabrics that you can find nowadays in all different price ranges.

It's time to listen to your senses when it comes to getting dressed and take this opportunity to portray your unique approach in life.

CREATIVE

Physical attributes

You have a very youthful energy and physique. Everybody thinks you're younger than you are. Your complexion is fine, and you radiate magic. Your bone structure is also fine, and your height is usually shorter than average. Your eyes may look a bit more pointy, and you'll have a magical/fairy vibe.

Personality and style

If you're reading this book, it's highly likely that you have some of this Personality Style in your profile.

Dear Creative, as your name says, your creativity is the one thing that keeps you alive! You daydream like you breathe! And you need others in your life to bring you down to planet Earth. You forget things all the time. Cooking or organising are just not your thing, you live in the world of dreams, and anything that has to do with 3D is just not your priority.

Usually, you have Romantic friends who will take care of you, otherwise you naturally wouldn't even think of eating.

You're a joy to be around and have a happy and upbeat personality. Your eyes shine bright, and you love expressing your magical internal world on the outside through art, your clothes or any other manner.

Self-expression is a big thing for you. You need it to feel alive in this 3D world. Wearing fantasy patterns, long butterfly/goddess dresses, and unique accessories, that's very much you.

You love colour in your clothes and organisational skills might not blend well with you.

Your ideal house would be full of art and symbolic items.

What to look for
- Look for garments that express who you feel you are on the inside. Sometimes that'll be an accessory. Sometimes it will be the whole outfit.
- Light and airy fabrics harmonise with your energy and complexion beautifully.
- Have fun with colour! Yours, out of all the Personality Styles, can get away with the most exciting colour combinations and

still look amazing.

- I especially love uniquely designed pieces for you. Look for artistic fashion and unique designs that align with your unique essence.

BALANCED YIN AND YANG ENERGY

CLASSIC

Physical attributes

The one physical characteristic that most aligns with your personality is symmetry and proportion. You aren't tall or short, you aren't big or small, your facial features aren't bigger or smaller than the others. You're right in the middle. Just like your personality, your physique isn't any of the extremes either.

Personality and style

You love safe, predictable, classic styles. You love order and organisation. Your ideal shoes are classic pumps or brogues. Pants with darts are your thing, whereas activewear is a big stretch. Sweating isn't something you enjoy.

Your tone of voice is mellow and correct. For you, the most important thing when getting dressed is structure, and it's normal for you to dress more formally than the average person might.

Your wardrobe is full of classic pieces, and you feel in complete disconnection with any type of creative activity. Your language is perfect, and you don't deal well with mess. Your style isn't boring. It's your style, and it's perfect for you, so stop trying to "innovate" if it doesn't feel authentic. The most precious gift you can give to yourself right now is to listen to your instincts and choose what feels right.

What to look for
- High quality, beautifully created, structured pieces.
- Neat hair and classic makeup (if applicable).
- Old-time classic pieces that'll never get old, like basic white shirts, classic pumps or brogues, high-quality leather accessories with minimum detail.
- Understand that structure is part of who you are; the more you use it in your clothes, the more your unique approach in life will be highlighted.
- Focus on neutrals and colours that align with your serene and peaceful nature. You don't have to pretend to be someone you aren't when you dress.

NATURAL

Physical attributes
Your next-door neighbour vibe is what defines you at its best. You aren't especially tall, normally leaning towards the shorter heights. Your carefree hair and athletic body are the most characteristic aspects of your body that allow you to enjoy your bush walks and trekking.

Personality and style
My dear Natural, you're a lover of comfort and ease. You're transparent and straightforward. You like things simple and clear. I love so much your passion for ethics and human rights. You're a fan of easy, care-free style.

Your fabrics need to be breathable and allow space for you to move: cotton, wool, wooden accessories, all from ethical brands that align with your values. Wearing accessories with elements of nature or knit are your thing.

Heels and full-on makeup are not for you, but you adapt to anything if it's necessary to meet people halfway.

An easy style for you is a pair of leggings with a knitted dress and short boots. A more masculine version of this might be a good quality cotton t-shirt or nice textured shirt with natural coloured pants.

Your best hairstyle is the one that requires least maintenance.

If you're reading this book and attracted to me, there's a high possibility that you're a Natural, as warm Creatives and Naturals are the types of clients I attract the most, as my personality is highly compatible with yours. I love simplicity and saying things in the simplest way I can without ulterior motives or hidden meaning.

Your ideal house is a wooden house in the woods, and you enjoy being a thrifter.

What to look for
- Natural fabrics, ethically made.
- Comfortable pieces that also make you feel attractive and expansive.
- Short boots, Salt-Water sandals, Birkenstocks, nature-inspired sneakers are shoes that would feed your soul.

- In general, pieces that allow your carefree nature to shine while making you feel abundant and powerful.

YANG ENERGY PREDOMINANCE

DRAMATIC

Physical attributes

Your striking appearance will make it easy to see that you have even a small part of this Personality Style in play.

You're generally tall and long, with straight facial features and a straight body shape. Your hair is also straight, very possibly dark, and your shoulders are square.

Personality and style

You love attention. Ambition is the one word that defines you. You love drama in your looks. You go for solid patterns (the black +red + white combo is big for you because of its striking contrast that harmonises with your inside-out nature) as well as monochromatic looks.

Pointy shoes go with your style as well as your features, which can be angular. You love statement pieces, and you don't hesitate to go big with just one item.

You love steel, black and/or red in your house. You're not usually into cooking or anything that means taking care of others. You're here to achieve and get things done, not waste time.

Your mind is always on the highest price tag items.

What to look for

- Straight designs that harmonise with your body shape.
- Inundate your closet with stiff fabrics and structured pieces.
- High-quality pieces and excellent confection will match your energy.
- Adding dramatic accessories will align with the aspect of you that's ready to set a statement everywhere you go.

ELEGANT SPORTY

Physical attributes

Your bone structure is larger than average. You lean towards the tall side. Your innate elegant vibe exudes presence and authority, but in a noble way, like old royalty.

Personality and Style

You're the one who's got an innate aura embedded in elegance. It doesn't matter what you wear. You just look elegant no matter what. You're a lover of traditions, and family is a high value of yours.

You look like you come from a family in a good level or from aristocracy, and you love quality. That's your thing. You'll use elbow patches just to keep using that checked blazer of yours.

You don't enjoy lavish things or ostentatious luxury. You appreciate beauty, culture, tradition and history.

All the pieces your wear are normally leaning to classic combined with comfort. You need space to move. You love wearing blazers, high boots, shirts, basic good quality jewellery. It's common to see you wearing loafers. Also, a vest and a tie or a thick blazer are very you, particularly if you are male.

You value your family lineage and enjoy things done properly.

Your ideal house is a big castle or *"finca"* where you have horses and dogs. You may also love a fireplace in your home.

What to look for
- High-quality, classic pieces that allow you to move.
- Comfortable fabrics that last.
- Thicker fabrics and textures are part of your ideal outfits, as they harmonise with your bigger bone structure.
- Blazers, high boots, loafers, ballerinas, plain white shirts, gold (yellow or white), high-quality leather bag or suitcase that is classic and charming at the same time.

FINAL NOTES ON PERSONALITY STYLES

In case you haven't got this message yet, energy *never* lies!

The more we're aware of it, the more freedom we achieve and the easier it becomes to translate it into clothes!

We all have a combo of each of these styles, but some people will have more feminine (yin energy or right-brain tendency), some will have more yang energy (yang or more left brain energy), and some will be in the middle between the two energies (balanced).

Unlike our colours, our Personality Style does evolve as we do! Having this resource will help you go back to it as a reference and better understand where your style is heading, then honour it with your clothes.

Your Unique Personality Style and your S.T.Y.L.E. Identity are not related, but you might find some answers on how your S.T.Y.L.E. Identity has been limiting you now that you have more information on your true essence. Now is a good time to shift it and embrace your true personality.

CHAPTER EIGHT

The visual game*

At the beginning of this book, I asked you to trust and relax. That was mainly because, in this part of the book, you won't find any pictures or style examples, and that's different to what you might have seen before. In fact, you won't find any cookie-cutter style advice. This is done purposely for one reason: to allow you to create your own version of this Visual Game.

We're all unique, and I don't have the right to define what your soul wants in any way.

What I *can* do, though, is show you how the visual game of style goes and guide you to radiate your pure light in your own way. This can be lots of fun if you allow it to be. Remember, you create your reality.

STYLE IS A VISUAL GAME

Before I explain this method of getting dressed, the method I use myself and with clients every day, I want to give you a heads up. I'm in this world to lead you in this transformation and show you what goes into my style method. You might, at some point, want to look for the complexity of it all. Before you do, let me tell you it is going to be simple.

Style is no more than a visual game. When you learn the little tricks that allow you to be on top of it, then you won't ever feel the frustration again.

In short, any outfit you wear has colours, textures and details that one way or another allow the eye to travel in different directions.

This eye movement is behind the effects that clothes will create when you see yourself wearing them.

When you become aware of how the eye travels, then you're set to win this game of clothes, and it will become fun... even addictive!

In the visual game, the ultimate objective is to draw the eye up to reach your face. Your job is to make it easy for the eye to do that and understand that it matters if the eye stops travelling!

Your face is your highest body part and the ultimate protagonist when it comes to dressing your body. The faster the eye travels upwards, the taller you'll look. That's because the eye will stop less on the way up. The opposite is also true. You'll look shorter if the eye travels slower, which happens when the eye stops more.

Isn't this the ultimate tribute to yourself? Years ago, money mentor Denise Duffield Thomas told me something that would change the way I looked at my face for good. I heard this at a time when I was feeling hesitant about *showing up too much* on social media. Denise uses the phrase:

"My face is my money."

Here's what I took from that. Your face is what helps you create that unique connection to others. It's the part of your body where you'll reflect your emotions and communicate.

The fact that I'm helping you make it easy for others to direct the eye towards your face, the ultimate expression of your soul – and no, we're not talking about physical appearance – is one more way for you to understand that this goes deeper. Your face is what will ultimately help you "make the money", make that connection with others. The more harmony you create with it, the more magnetic and attractive you'll be.

Show that face of yours unapologetically and what others will see is the powerful energy you bring to the table.

So, what attracts the eye? Colours, details, lines, hems... Anything that breaks the space in your outfit.

Every single 'stop' your eye makes when travelling is a spot that will automatically bring attention to the area. Wherever you place your attention, it expands, and this happens with your eye too. Wherever your eye stops, the area will visually expand.

You can *choose* how many times you want the eye to stop, and you can choose where. I'm going to help you understand how to choose wisely.

So, what 'stops' would I choose for eye travel? What factors influence how the eye travels and how can we use them to our advantage?

THE COLOUR FACTOR

Generally, we find that: light colours and bright colours expand and bring attention; dark colours and muted colours recede and disguise.

You can use this to your advantage by placing such colours where you want to highlight or otherwise. The more contrast there is in your outfits, the louder the attention will be, so choose wisely where you want that attention to go.

Here's a simple example of this in practice:

Let's say you're wearing an all-black outfit, and the only colour you add is red in a pair of red shoes. Unless you add another red detail to the area around your head, the eye will have a hard time travelling up to your face. What will the result be? An outfit that's not making *you* the protagonist, but the shoes.

Instead, if you were to add any detail – say red lipstick, earrings, a handkerchief, anything that helps to bring the eye upwards and make the most of your amazing body and face – then the outfit will be complete because it's making the eye's journey so much easier starting from the bottom and travelling upwards until the next colour that breaks the monotony.

If you decide to have only one bright/light colour, make sure it's at the top half of your body and ideally as close to your face as possible. There's a reason why monochromatic outfits are the big secret of shorter figures as it allows the eye to travel without stopping, making it easier to create a visually longer figure.

If you want to create volume in the area of your buttocks, use lighter/brighter colours and contrast with your top-level to do it. If you want to bring attention to your top area, try to use colours that won't catch so much attention on your bottom half.

Knowing how each colour type impacts the eye, you can make decisions to your benefit! By choosing colours from the better half of the colour spectrum, your colour palette, you're guaranteed success in playing this game. Yes, as I said, it's *that* simple.

THE DETAILS FACTOR

Details can be the one tool you get good at, and that gives you the results you've always wanted. Anything can be a detail. And *any* detail whatsoever brings attention, which means your eye travels towards it. That creates two optical effects: it makes the area larger, and it helps the eye travel in the direction you want.

This is a fun and powerful bit of information that can transform your outfits!

The higher you place details on your figure, the higher your eye will travel. The fewer details you have in your outfit, the less the eye will stop, therefore, the longer the optical image will be and vice versa.

I've said details can be anything, but to get you started, here's what I mean: lipstick, tie length, tie knot, rise, pockets, hems, pattern, accessories, buttons... The list goes on. Any single item that breaks the space can be considered a detail.

THE LINES FACTOR

Whenever I show people in my workshops this one trick, attendees go: "Ooooohhh!!"

Stand in front of a mirror, pull your sleeve to your waist and take a picture. Then pull your sleeve up to the level of your breasts and take a picture. Then pull it up as much as you can – to the widest part of your biceps – and take a picture.

Wherever the horizontal line of your sleeve falls, the area appears bigger. Yes, lines are that powerful!

Where your sleeve hem falls, the eye stops, making the area look bigger. There you have breast-, bicep-, or hip-expansion for free.

Now you know why it looks better when you put on a t-shirt or top and turn over the hem (or pull it down) or why you prefer one type of sleeve than another. This is how to play with hem lengths visually to balance your body height and different widths.

So, if you want your legs to look longer, shorten your jeans or even tuck them in a bit. When we show skin, the legs appear longer. By being able to see your ankle, you create an instant lengthening effect. Sarah Jessica Parker, with a petite figure, is known for wearing Ugg boots and showing her ankles even in freezing cold New York for that same reason.

Now, think about what you can do to play with lines!

Do vertical or diagonal lines (only the ones who move upwards in the direction we read) do the opposite then? Of course! You just have to be careful if you have a curvy body because too many lines can be contradictory. (More on this in the Harmony section coming up.)

Vertical lines can be part of your patterns, but you can also add them with layers like jackets or vests, for instance.

CONTRASTING VOLUME

Keep in mind: the looser and bigger the difference between the skirts/sleeve/short hem width with your leg/arm width, the narrower your leg/arm will look and vice versa.

That's why you see men showing off muscle with tight sleeves and women showing off curves with tight and short dresses.

HIGHLIGHT AND DISGUISE

Now that you know how you can use details and colours wisely, you're ready to learn my highlighting and disguising principle, a mind shift that'll help you keep a positive focus when it comes to dressing your sacred body every day. Ready?

Always focus on highlighting your asset(s), the areas you like about yourself the most, over camouflaging your least favourite areas (if there are any). Anything counts as an asset! Face, eyes, hair, butt, breasts, arms, you name it.

The reason this principle was born is because I too often saw people so self-conscious and focused on camouflaging certain areas that they missed their *golden* attributes that were just screaming to be shown off!

Let's say you're a woman, and you have some volume in the midriff, and you decide to put a black, straight tunic on in order to camouflage it. (The amount of times I've seen this happening is outrageous!) Instead, what if you *first* focused on the beautiful waist you have or your cleavage or your lips? Some men tend to let their little amount of hair grow, so they camouflage their baldness, but what if I told you I find bald men sexy? What if you *first* focused on highlighting your amazing personality or certain features with the right colours?

There's no wrong answer when it comes to where you openly or secretly feel proud. Nobody needs to know. Just you and this book. It'll be our secret trick to transform the way you show up unapologetically, inner-outer connected and inexplicably powerful and attractive on the outside from all the abundance and expansion you're embodying in all its shapes and forms.

Do you know what happens when you highlight *first*? The magic that's created when you focus on highlighting all your beautiful attributes is that you'll most likely have *already* done the camouflaging job. Yes. Because the eye will want to travel to the highlighted areas, it will pass over the areas you don't want noticed!

So, once more, it's all about how you want to interpret life, including your amazing body, and picking the magic lane will get the most stunning results for you.

HARMONY

First things first. There is *no* such thing as body shape. Rather than classifying your body shape with a cookie-cutter system, I'm going to help you understand how *harmony* is the natural tendency to follow when it comes to styling your unique body pattern.

I find this aspect of style delightful. Don't let the perfectionist in you get caught up in 3D standards, but rather let yourself tune into this: 70% perfection is 100% success.

You can find harmony in so many ways. Rather than trying to specify a shape for your body, stand in front of the mirror and observe any predominant patterns:

Look at your facial features and your body lines. Do you see more curves or straight lines? Is your lower body wider than the top? Or is your top wider than your bottom? Are they just the same? (If you can't tell, that's probably not an aspect you need to focus on.) Are there a lot of curves on your face?

Whether you see straight lines or curves will align with your Unique Personality Style (yin-yang-balanced). You will find harmony by replicating this as much as you can in your clothes and accessories because one way of highlighting your personality and bringing out the best of your features is by focusing on them and honouring them.

The important message here is to go with the flow. Instead of fighting your nature, honour it. Instead of trying to hide what you feel self-conscious about, focus on the beauty of your unique features and search for inspiration within you. Use colour and harmony to balance and highlight whatever you want.

Decide where you want to add volume and where you don't – both physically and visually with colour and details. Don't fixate on shape, but rather on using the Visual Game to make the most of what you have.

You can highlight curves by harmonising with them and dressing them with fabrics that follow them, patterns that also have curves, details like accessories, pockets, collars with the same type of lines that you naturally own, and the same will apply for straight lines.

BONE STRUCTURE

Following your own design also includes how thick or thin your bone structure might be. This is key for you to understand why some fabrics might look funny on you and vice versa, like you looking bigger when wearing them or like they're taking over.

We achieve greater balance when we match the heaviness of our bone structure to the weight of the fabrics and accessories we wear.

Someone with a larger bone structure, for instance, usually has bigger wrists and a wider frame, but there are many versions of this. As an example, I have a medium to big bone structure, and I know this because I look funny in very thin fabrics. My wrists are normal, not thick, but my bone structure has always been bigger than average. As I grew up, that knowledge could have come in pretty handy being already in a woman's body and trying to wear flimsy, itty-bitty clothes made for girls.

If you have a delicate structure, you could paint yourself with thin strokes on a canvas, whereas somebody with a larger structure would be painted with a thicker stroke.

Another major reason I've included this aspect in the Visual Game is so that you are aware when it comes to accessories, as thicker, heavier-looking accessories will harmonise best with larger bone structures and vice versa. That applies to bags, belt buckles, jewellery, anything really.

TEXTURE

I find this aspect of harmony fascinating.

Dictionary definition of texture:

> The *quality* of something that can be *known* by *touch*; the *degree* to which something is *rough* or *smooth* or *soft* or *hard*.

Now, when we're talking about fabrics and accessories, this sounds like an easy way to classify them, right? It's also a smart way to notice how certain types of materials align with you more than others. The reason? Harmony!

When it comes to texture in people, we can determine that by the hair, the look of the skin, freckles and so on. Somebody with curly voluminous hair would have texture, but that doesn't mean their face would have texture. They might have smooth skin.

Noticing all these details in you can help you feel inspired to choose certain textures or combinations of textures. It's like the cherry on top but also a highly comforting aspect of the art of dressing from an energetic perspective.

And that's it! That is all you need to turn 180 degrees in the direction of your true style.

The question now is:

Are you ready to take responsibility and make it happen?

It's time to create space for your transformation!

STYLE POWER

CHAPTER NINE

Dare to dress in a way that's true to you*

Here's the truth. Pushing to the edge of our warm and cosy comfort zone is bloody hard. Fear of the unknown keeps us humans stuck – too often for too long.

Personally speaking, I have reached a point where standing for too long in my comfort zone feels uncomfortable because I know that's a synonym for not growing.

When it comes to the work in this book, you might say *I don't even know where to start* or a straight *I don't want to change*. And that's alright. Just remember this resistance is expected and normal, but I know you can do this.

We can use clothes to look at our approach to safety and as a way to start getting out of our comfort zone. What if you woke up tomorrow and decided to add a little component of fun into your outfit? Go on! I dare you!

CONTAGIOUS HARMONY

"Look at them. I want some of that!"

This is the common reaction triggered in someone when they see you embodying harmony. Harmony makes this process an intuitive one.

At the end of the day, we all just want to have our "stuff" together. From the outside, when you take care of only your external style, others might say you look good, but it gets to a point where that's unsustainable for you. You can't fake it forever. When harmony comes from the inside and your transformation expresses itself from your inner work, that's when the harmony becomes contagious in a good way.

When you exude harmony, people will feel compelled and attracted to what you're doing. You become not only stylish but magnetic. Your work reaches further dimensions. You're not here to paint a perfect picture on the outside. You're here to live your truth. And that, my friend, is the most powerful place you can operate from.

Those people you'll attract who want some of what you've got will also benefit from that inner-outer harmony of yours and will want more of that for themselves.

LIVE YOUR LIFE, NOBODY ELSE'S

My current version of living *your* life is believing your life is the one you've created. For that reason, it's time to embrace it, show up and take responsibility. Setting your eye on the prize, where do you want to go from here? What do you want to create? Listen. What does your light say? Follow that.

Living your life fully means not settling for less. This is a lesson I'm still learning. Having tried so hard for so long to be the good girl nobody would know, this is a muscle that I need to stretch everyday. The easy call? Not reaching out. Not speaking up. Settling for less.

But I'm a connector. I thrive by connecting authentically with real people who might have different points of view but always come from pure heart. That's my focus as I'm writing this book. I want to connect with you.

As one of my mentors says, "F***ing live your life!"

And I want to add, "And dress for it!"

HOW DO YOU WANT TO FEEL?

As a woman raised in a traditional family in Spain, leaving the house in activewear was definitely not an option for me. Even being at home in activewear wasn't something I enjoyed.

Now, with two little ones, I'm playing, jumping on the trampoline, running, dancing and rolling around on the floor all the time. Many days, I live in my activewear, and I love it.

The thing is it's not just any activewear. I choose carefully how I want to feel at home, and a pair of pants from Target won't make the cut if I'm going to feel the way I want to feel.

Are you a feeler? Do you wake up in the morning, and before you choose anything, ask yourself, *How would I like to feel?* Are you more of a practical person and ask yourself what you have to do today and then just wear what's convenient for it? Maybe you think about the weather or who you're going to meet.

Whatever comes to your mind, do yourself a favour and always end your internal dialogue with, *How do I want to feel about today's timetable?* That'll determine your future decisions about when to add a new piece to your closet, such as new activewear.

Remember, it's not what you wear, but how you feel when you wear it. It doesn't matter what you wear. It really doesn't. What matters are the emotions, feelings, thoughts that run through your system when you wear your favourite piece of clothing. Wouldn't you pay a substantial amount of money to feel like *that* in every single item you wear, even your pyjamas?

Well, it's just a matter of setting a standard and deciding how much you're willing to give up to set your (closet) boundaries! How high are your expectations for dressing you? Then it's just a matter of asking the Universe and acting in accordance; in other words, making it happen.

"But Alma", I hear you say, "What about money blocks?" I hear you on that one. Here's a big truth on that one. They're 100% tied to your self-worth.

There are many ways to work on money blocks, but realise that all the work you do on self-worth will be positively reflected in your money situation, as you'll believe in how deserving you are versus how much you deserve debt. (Ha! Careful with that one.)

Pay attention to what you focus on. Is it on what you lack or how you want to feel?

MAINTAINING THE MAKEOVER

I used to love helping my friends and family with their wardrobe, hair and makeup all the time.

I remember watching a TV show years ago about makeovers. I was at home in Spain, and I remember like it was yesterday how the participants described how they felt before and after.

That's amazing, I thought at first, *this is exactly what I want: to help people to make the most of what they have.*

Years passed, and I became an image consultant. That's when I realised there was a difference between fixing people and bringing out the best in them. Those participants went under the most invasive treatments to be completely transformed, and that part of the show is what turned me off. I wouldn't suggest surgery to anybody. Hair, makeup, wardrobe? Yes. Further than that is not my zone. That doesn't mean I don't approve of it. Who am I to judge what others do with their body?

Going back to the TV show, when I saw the end result, it dawned on me that these people feel amazing now, and that's awesome. There's just one big "but"...

How are they going to maintain those looks? The hair was done, make up was done, the outfit was on. Who has time for that on the daily? I certainly don't, and neither do those who feel called to work with me. For me, the real makeover happens when you feel the change so deeply on the inside that you consistently show up changed and your whole reality follows. It's *not* about fixing or trying to live up to exterior standards. It's about enhancing who you are, connecting with your true essence.

Doing this on a daily basis, then making it a way of being, a lifestyle, that's the point. I've had clients who have even dyed their bed sheets a year after going through my course because that's how energetically connected they felt to their colour palette.

The big question here is not whether you want to look good or stylish or appropriate for any occasion. We all want to look good. The big question is whether you want to look and feel good and make it your reality.

If the answer is yes you do, then I believe you're in the best place and in the best hands. From right now, *your* choices are the best anybody can make in your life because you are the one who is making them.

Okay, pep talk done. Next up, I'm going to give you a little more insight into my experience with the Style Power Formula and how to implement it.

CHAPTER TEN

Self-discovery and dressing from the inside out in my experience*

CONFIDENCE IS ALSO ABOUT LOVE

People say I'm a confident person and I say I'm a great actress because I don't always feel confident. It took a long time for me to see my true self in the mirror. I armed myself with the right tools to remind me how much I value myself, even on days when my mind might be playing tricks on me. In other words, I choose to be confident.

Our deepest essence, our highest self, only knows about loving ourselves. We learned not to love ourselves as we grew up and *"comparisonitis"* has a lot to say on this matter. So just like everybody, I have days where I have many doubts.

In the past, I wasn't that compassionate with others. I believed this was because I had even less compassion towards myself. Here's what I've learned through the years. What you do on the outside is no more and no less than a reflection of the relationship you have with yourself. And yes, that can be a strong slap in the face.

Once, I heard from Eckhart Tolle a very good interpretation of what Jesus said on the cross that made me understand how true compassion works:

Father, forgive them, for they do not know what they do.
LUKE 23:34

What I think he meant was: they're doing the best they can from what they know! Whaaaaaat?

So, if ever I was not nice to you, I apologise. I was being far worse to myself on the inside. We learn so many lessons after we cross over the barrier to self-love and acceptance.

"Don't be fooled by the rocks that I got." This is one challenge I've experienced and still experience in my own human skin. It's why I believe this is my dharma: to reclaim all my power, to love myself unconditionally no matter what the scale says, what I choose to wear or how long it takes me to reach a target.

There are good days, and then there are days when I don't even look in the mirror because I need to not feed the head trash. Some days, we just have to be gentle to ourselves and understand that we're not in the right space to look ourselves in the mirror. And that's so okay, my friend, so okay!

My husband thinks I'm the most beautiful woman. When I started dating him, I showed up believing what he said. I was 27, and I wasn't anywhere near feeling confident with my looks. He didn't understand that I'd set my own bar so low when it came to self-perception, probably from years of feeling like a nobody in school.

Even though leaving my hometown in Mallorca at age 23 to finish my bachelor's degree in Barcelona gave me a great boost as far as discovering my limiting beliefs, it still took several years to believe that I was beautiful, no matter what, I was loved, no matter what, and that I was smart, no matter what.

All in all, it took a lot to build up my confidence to where it is now.

STEPS TO SELF-DISCOVERY

I admire women who seem to have it all figured out. They stand so firmly to their values, their boundaries are impeccable, and they're compassionate people at heart. Yet, on the inside, they probably feel very similar to how you and I do. We're all living a human life.

To be okay on the days when I didn't feel strong, I built a closet around me. From that place, I'd remind myself, *Psssst! Remember? We love ourselves now. And this is the proof: enjoy choosing what to wear.*

A while ago, somebody who I thought was a friend, even though my gut told me she wasn't, said to me, "You're weak."

It hit me hard because I had opened all my insecurities to this person, and I wasn't expecting somebody to tell me that. Especially after becoming a mother! That wasn't how I felt, and it was an important wake-up call for me.

We are whatever we choose to be. If we don't rise, those who don't know better will take the opportunity to step on us. And it's our choice if we allow that to happen.

When that toxic relationship was over, I rose so much higher. I realised how much garbage we can tell ourselves just because we don't have the right people around us.

I didn't get here overnight. Looking back, here are the stages I went through on my journey to discover my sense of self:

Step #1:
GETTING RID OF THOSE WHO DIDN'T ADD TO MY LIFE

Sometimes we can't just remove people from our life, but we can leave them out of our system, by setting boundaries, honouring ourselves, our time and our most precious energy, and accessing as much personal power we can.

I've become quite an expert in energetically withdrawing from those who don't feel in tune with my journey at a specific time. The important part is to do it lovingly, which is something I'm still working on. On the inside, I might still try to find answers on why others behave a certain way, but then that's not compassion, is it? I realised it's not staying in a state of peace and retaining my power.

Step #2:
FINDING OUT HOW TO DRESS IN A WAY THAT HONOURS ME

When I started in this industry to help others, I was the one who needed help the most. This challenge was sent to me so that I could pass it on to others in turn. I see that now.

At the time, though, my total disconnection from who I was and my low confidence wouldn't let me see that this work I was doing was to save *me*, and then, through my journey, share all I had learned.

I used to spend an hour easily in front of a closet full of clothes and still feel

I had nothing to wear. Nothing would look good on me. Why did I think that? Because I only saw flaws. Not a single good trait. On good days, if I had the impression that I had lost some weight, I may have felt on the slightly higher side of low self-worth, but that was about it.

The process of knowing my body and appreciating my traits internally and externally in order to highlight them was pretty much life-changing.

Looking at myself through the eyes of love instead of using the critical lenses I had learned, that was truly something.

The tools I share today and have shared throughout *Style Power* are the ones I've arrived at after years of refining my processes. I've finally come to determine the true methods that I use every day and that help me create the outfits I love most.

Even though helping others discover and dress themselves has helped me, I didn't truly get to know my inner self and love her until I sat with myself.

Step #3:
SITTING WITH MYSELF

Only a couple of years ago did I finally come to realise that I needed to sit with myself, listen to my self-talk and nourish the relationship I had with myself. Meditating and feeling a sense of how good it feels inside my body and doing self-hypnosis so that I could see myself at peace and worthy helped a lot. I envisioned myself surrounded by abundance and love in all its forms.

All those tools led me to have a sense of self and a willingness to expand and help others expand that I never in my life would have thought to experience without them. Most importantly, I gained a feeling of being part of the *whole*, of how much personal power I have and of my ever-present connection to the source that created it all.

Am I at the end of this journey?
Definitely not.

Do I have it all figured it out?
Most definitely not.

I believe life is all about celebrating milestones. The beauty is in the journey, which is basically our life. Of course, reaching goals needs to be celebrated, but that tends to happen only at certain times. You don't want to live in a state of feast and famine when it comes to being grateful and cherishing those ordinary moments and everyday milestones that you keep achieving too.

IF YOU WERE YOUR BEST FRIEND...

This is what I tell my eldest son every time he gets annoyed and calls himself names:

"You're your best friend."

Normally I ask, "How would you feel if somebody called you the names that you call yourself when getting frustrated?"
"Bad," he says.
"Would you like to be around that friend?"
"No, he wouldn't be my friend," he replies.

As always, my son is a mirror for me and nothing less. When I go through this with him, I recognise I need to up-level my own game.
We can't expect others to treat us better than we treat ourselves. Let's learn the lesson once and for all. We are responsible for what we keep in our

lives, and it's up to us to connect to what makes us come alive from the inside. Even though it's hard to understand sometimes, I believe we come to this life with a soul contract to fulfil and have the power to create what we need.

Nobody will enter your inner cave and tell you that you need to tidy it up. It's up to you to pick up your dirty socks and put them in the laundry pile. You must be that person for yourself. You must be your own best friend, period.

Style Power Practice
BE YOUR OWN BEST FRIEND

Here are some reflection questions for you to sink into this idea of being your own best friend.

If you were your best friend:

How would you treat yourself?
How would you dress yourself?
How would you feed yourself?
What would you say to yourself?
How much time would you want to enjoy with yourself?
How much would you enjoy your company?

Some people say, "But I don't like being alone." But being alone is just a perception. You're never truly alone. You're part of the whole. We all are. That's where the saying we're one gets its meaning. It's why the answer to all questions is found within because we belong to a higher dimension that we can't comprehend.

Whenever I need to answer a big question, my first thought is still:

> Who can help me answer this?
> Who can help me figure out what I'm supposed to do with my life?
> Who can help me move forward with my business?
> Who can help me know what to do with my kids?

When we're able to achieve that sense of self and discover our inner world, all those questions are answered in one place. It's not like we need to try hard. Those answers just come. Maybe you'll be going for a walk or peeling potatoes in the kitchen. (Yep, I get many downloads that way!) All the answers are found in the same place, and you can access them anytime because that place is *you*.

DO IT FOR YOU

Who are you transforming for? Unless you care a whole lot about satisfying yourself (yes, I'm talking about style, but you apply it to anything you want), you'll *never* feel like you're nailing this style game.

During my first year in the image consulting industry, I was approached by a client who hired me for a whole style assessment and personal shopping package. I always interview people before starting our work together to see if we're a good fit. The one thing that felt off was that this client wanted to do the "makeover" to make her ex-boyfriend jealous and choose her over the new woman he was seeing. This is clear proof of how lost I was when

I started and how much I needed to learn because I said yes to working with her.

Needless to say, the whole process was a disaster. She was highly displeased with the shopping services, and the whole experience was just plain bad. I learned so many lessons, the first of which was never never never undercharge! Secondly, don't try to help anybody who is being motivated from the outside, no matter how much they pay.

Whatever I did for that client, it would never have been enough because that person needed to love herself enough to not need anybody else's approval rather than trying to dress in a way that affected others!

When we're little, we're taught to be good girls and tough men; somewhere in between those cliches, we lose the potential of self-reassurance. It's so ingrained in our brain that it can take many years to realise this whole journey isn't about others' opinions of us but about our relationship with ourselves, knowing ourselves and understanding how we can serve others.

So, ask yourself this question:

Who am I doing this for?

You don't need to focus on an answer. Just focus on opening the energy to do this for yourself. Not for your husband, not for your wife, not for a date...

For you.

If you can't find a place within you where you want to do this for yourself, this whole process won't be sustainable, it won't make any sense, and it will be a huge waste of time

*

Implementing The Style Power Formula

*

STYLE POWER

CHAPTER ELEVEN

Adapting your reality to support your connection with your closet*

It's time to bring to your awareness some of my practical strategies that will help you implement the Style Power Formula in the most successful way. That wardrobe is not going to align to your essence by itself! It's time to take some action in this reality. Here I'm going to share some tips for getting it done in the most flawless way.

DECLUTTERING

At some point on your style journey, as you align more with yourself and create a wardrobe that shows on the outside who you are on the inside, you're probably going to find yourself needing to make some room – which means getting rid of things that no longer align with your sense of self or your vision.

It'll get to a point where, if you don't do this right away, you'll naturally start isolating pieces in your closet that aren't honouring you. The more you'll become aware of the energy behind those clothes that are honouring you, the more you'll want to stay in that zone. Once you start growing in that direction, this process will be part of your life until you end up with a closet that feels 100% aligned with your essence.

Let's make a start on how you might approach this (potentially) tricky exercise.

You'll want to get rid of whatever didn't make the cut in the Style Power Formula in terms of colour, style and personality.

It's time now to take action into this self-honouring journey and start taking physical steps towards that sacred connection to your body and your wardrobe.

Instead of getting into the right or wrong space, sit in a state of curiosity and observe how getting rid of pieces that you know aren't honouring you is costing you.

Say goodbye to the old to allow space and welcome the new. You can now say thank you and goodbye to any pieces that didn't make the cut in the Style Power Formula, whether that's because of colour, style or personality, including:

- Pieces that you haven't worn for the last two years.
- Anything torn, worn, or out of shape.
- Pieces that don't bring you joy, as Marie Kondo puts it, don't belong to your closet.
- And finally, those pieces that you *know* energetically don't belong to your closet. (You will develop this sense over time. Give yourself space to nurture this new and expansive relationship with your closet).

That's pretty much it!

If it gets too hard, you can always set aside some items and observe how you'll naturally want to get rid of them after some time focusing on the work inside this book. I bet you'll end up selling them or giving them to charity before too long!

If you still don't feel a shift, look at what is making you feel so attached to those pieces. Remember, we come and leave this planet without anything. Consider this... Is that wardrobe supporting you at your best during this journey?

Every step of this process brings you an opportunity to grow and increase your self-awareness. Decluttering is no different!

FILTER-SHOPPING

I'm a fast shopper. I *love* shopping fast. One of my best friends always remembers how awesome it was going shopping with me. Back in the pre-kids, pre-corporate days, I'd go for a walk with him, and we'd get to a store I wanted to go in. The first time that happened, he dreaded what would happen. What he didn't know was I've always hated spending too much time in stores. I try to be in there in little increments of time only.

The reason why is my energy drops in shops. As an empath, I'm sensitive to energy, and crowded stores are the least appealing of all places. I became a master in the art of fast and effective shopping. Even though I love buying online and I'm grateful to live in an era when that's actually a thing, I have to go in shops sometimes because I love touching fabrics and holding garments.

If you find shopping as draining as I do, here's the good news: with the style tools I've shared with you, spotting the right pieces will take only a fraction of the time that it used to take you. And the more you follow the Style Power Formula, the faster you'll become at heading for the items that work best for you.

If you've come this far in the book, chances are you're not the same person as when you started reading. For starters, your standards aren't the same, so there are many stores you'll naturally discard just from the act of touching fabric and holding garments.

Let me go through the filtering process with you, so you can picture how magical this new way of shopping is.

Your number one filter is colour. This is visual, so you can quickly scan stores and decide if you're going to spend time in there or not. Because yes, you have that choice, ha! Also, can we acknowledge that we live in lucky times where we can shop online? When you're shopping online, it's even easier, as there's usually a function where you can filter items by colour.

Once you spot pieces in the colours you're looking for, then it's just a matter of seeing if you can find what you're looking for. That means the following filters are things like:

> Is the fabric flowy or stiff?
> Is the pattern right for your features?
> Will it make the most of your figure?
> What do you need to look for that harmonises with you?
> Do you love it?
> Is it worth your precious time to try it on?

Not so long ago, my middle sister came shopping with me and was in shock. In a one-hour "walk" around my hometown in Palma, I found like four pieces that I absolutely loved, and they were the only ones I tried. That's how accurate you're going to get.

Of course, I often try pieces where I have low expectations that they'll suit me. Sometimes they don't work, and that's okay. This is only on days when

I'm truly in the mood to shop, in need of some retail therapy to distract myself or when I can force myself to get out and have some fun.

Disclaimer: On those days, I rarely buy something. I've reached a place where I rarely shop for something I'm not going to wear or that doesn't belong in my closet. Shopping can't be a healthy gateway for any emotional crisis. Personally, for me, on low days, getting out of the house, working in a cafe and going for a browse in a couple of stores makes me realise I belong to a world full of people and that I love appreciating clothes.

Do I indulge sometimes? Of course! But here's the difference. In my opinion, when we're addicted to something, there's no system behind it. Addiction is a big word and it requires specific professional help. Let's not confuse concepts here. I don't treat shopping that way, and if you do, this isn't a book that'll help you get out of that state. However, if you want to understand what healthy, self-honouring, sustainable shopping can look like for you, you're in the right place.

The ultimate goal of a shopping spree is to familiarise yourself with what fits and to enjoy the process. When it becomes a sacrifice, the outcome won't and can't be the same!

A quick word on outlet shopping before we move on. Because of how quickly fashion moves nowadays, the awesome thing about outlets is you can find so many pieces to add to your basics. You just need to find the right outlets – both online and offline – to get the amazing value high-quality pieces at a fraction of the usual price.

PROGRESS NOT PERFECTION
That's the key to getting somewhere in this journey. When you're putting outfits together, don't get caught up too much in nailing the "no-rules"

approach you've learned in this book. Go with the flow. Try, fail, laugh. Let yourself enjoy the process. This is supposed to be fun. It's about discovering yourself and dressing for your self, remember. Shopping is just the tip of the iceberg, the cherry on top.

I actually get more out of seeing my clients in outfits that are "off" but that they look excited wearing because I see they're experimenting and learning. The idea of perfection is idealistic; you're *always* going to find a flaw if you look for it.

Go for improvement, not absolute results.

I see you wanting to get this right, and I ask you to let go of that. We're no longer going to work from that space. Let it flooooow.

If you buy pieces online, there's a good chance they might not look their best when you put them together for real, but with time you'll learn how to identify the right shapes and brands for you. It's a matter of starting *somewhere*, and first and foremost, being kind to yourself.

Hot tip: Always take pictures of your outfit and observe with the most loving eyes. If you're not sure, leave it and come back later or the next day to look at it with fresh eyes. Taking a picture can help you look at how your outfit honours you from a more objective point of view.

ENERGY AND FABRICS

As the magical Florence Scovel Shinn said in her book *The Game of Life*, "Never violate a hunch." In that same book, she tells the story of a man who had the gut feeling to spend all the money he had on a coat that was going to help him get into the vibration to attract more. And that's what happened!

There's a good reason why we feel next-level when we buy better quality. Like everything in this world, it's made up of subatomic particles that are charged. In other words, everything vibrates with its own energy, including the clothes you wear.

Higher quality means higher care on the garment, which will make it a better candidate to honour yourself, I invite you to think about it.

There are certain fabrics that carry a higher vibration than others, those that are closer to nature, least modified, more pure.

Note that there is a difference between quality and expensive. They don't always go hand-in-hand, and it's important to differentiate.

One of my many tricks to shopping online is to always check the price of a certain piece on more than one website. If you find that a piece is way cheaper in the country of the brand's origin, chances are that the quality isn't worth the price quoted in your country, so wait for a sale if you really like the piece. Of course, there are exceptions, but be smart and think about the margin that the retailer takes for that $1,000 coat. If you know that it'll be discounted at 80% by the end of the season, chances are there's a high mark-up, and the quality is not up to that price. If it's a $2,000 coat that won't go on sale until it reaches the high brand outlets in a year, if ever, then that item will probably be worth its quality-price ratio.

Price indications are only one factor of quality, and there are always exceptions, as I've said. This is just one general rule when making decisions on higher investment pieces.

If you're into budgets, this one's for you. Do your best to make the most of your yearly budget and buy pieces that *deserve* you. Ask your body what the right budget is for you, then add a bit more to push you into a slightly more abundant wardrobe than you think you deserve. You can start by moving to just the next level up in quality, and you can do this even if you buy in thrift stores.

LESS IS MORE

While we're on the subject of money, let me share this. One day, I observed what I was wearing taking Tom to school, and it hit me that I was asking for more from a place of not enough. I was asking for more from a perfectionist perspective. The thought process went like this:

"Once I have this in my closet, then I'll be happy. Once I have those leather pants, then it'll be great."

Truthfully, my wardrobe is *full* of awesome clothes that I had curated and chosen for myself over the years. That day, I was wearing a pair of Superga shoes, a Barbour jacket and a State of Escape bag. I noticed that this was an updated version of what those rich German women in Portals in Mallorca would wear. As a child, I would always look at them, admiring their natural sense of style and their beautiful clothes, which was completely unreachable to my 13-year-old self. More than 20 years later, I recognise that as an intention being created at just the right time.

When it comes to spending and clothes, believe you're worth spending money on high-quality items. Higher quality means longer life in your closet. And that means you'll buy fewer of them! For the sake of the planet, the smart strategy is spending only on things that are truly worth being in your closet; that's how I operate most of the time, and I believe that's the way to go! Now, I'd be a hypocrite if I told you that's what I do all the time, and that's what you should be doing. I do have days where I spend on pieces that might not be aligned to that, just so I don't spend too much on clothes that I know I won't feel like wearing for 10 years.

Likewise, I don't like to limit you and tell you you need five tops, three bottoms and one pair of shoes to create a capsule. (For my A-type goddesses, we do create capsules in my online program and private coaching. You can find out more about my latest offerings on my website www.almabarrero.com.) For now, this book is all about freedom. It's about you do you, and I'll give you what's worked for my many clients... as well as what hasn't!

As an idea of what to do to create a little capsule, see the chart below. This is totally customisable. You can add more tops, more jackets, more one-pieces like dresses, jumpsuits, etc.

Jacket/s	Top 1	Bottom 1	Accessories Shoes Bags
	Top 2		Suitcases Jewellery Scarves
	Top 3	Bottom 2	Coats Ties Belts etc.

And we fill it with clothes that mix and match, which is easy to do when you have identified your specific magic palette. However, simply knowing if you're warm and cool, most colours will match.

Get your own copy of this capsule chart at **www.stylepowerbook.com.**

The idea with a capsule wardrobe is, of course, to create outfits, so I highly recommend taking pictures or notes of the individual pieces and sticking them inside your closet door. This is how my hubby used to create his outfits when going to work. He loved doing it this way as he's all about systems and organisation. Likewise, all my Type-A clients find this method a life-saver.

Now, it's up to you if you want to create a capsule for each aspect of your lifestyle or one big one for everything. It really depends on the different things you do! My life, for example, is pretty much living in casual wear as I work from home and drop off the kids at school. I have a smaller selection of smart or elegant clothes for events and meetings. However, if you work in an office, it might look very different.

The whole idea of these capsules is to help those who want and need structure. You wake up in the morning, and all the work is done. You just need to choose what to wear from the capsule chart. It makes your style life so much simpler and more effective, that's for sure.

Now here's the thing. When you discover your magic palette, it becomes even easier to put pieces together, as most colours match perfectly.

All in all, though, know that however you do this wardrobe approach, it's the perfect way. Don't put too much time into it if it overwhelms you. I'm one of those people who gets lost in too much detail, so if that's the case for you, just go with the two premises that I've mentioned in this section. To recap, those are:

- Focusing on increasing quality and reducing quantity.
- Sticking to your magical palette (or as close as you can with the tools I'm providing you), so colours will automatically match!

CHAPTER TWELVE

Putting it all together and trusting the process *

So, let's say you've gone through the whole Style Power Formula process – you've connected with your sense of self, you've pinpointed your vision for yourself and your current identity (that may be holding you back), you've used the (Un)conventional Style Tools to start finding your best colours and identify style personality as well as you've learned some style principles to help you make the most of the sacred body you have. Now all you need is to find some clothes!

Whenever I need something to show up in my life, I use this fun little game, and we can apply it now to clothes and see if it works for you.

Style Power Practice
PLACE A DIVINE ORDER FOR THE PERFECT PANTS

Let's say that you're creating a capsule, and you need a pair of aubergine pants to go with your outfit. For the love of God, you can't find them, and you're wondering what the hell you're supposed to do now, right?

Okay, first of all, when you start dressing in the shades of your colour palette, it's a bit of an adjustment in the beginning. Instead of seeing this as a limit to your shopping freedom, look at it as freeing your soul to expand and feel joyful in a house decorated in harmony with your soul's energy.

Now that you've set yourself free, you just need the perfect piece to remind you of your freedom.

Then, order it from the Universe.

Here's what you say:

> *If it's in my best interest and highest good to find these aubergine pants <or specify item>, they will show up at the perfect time <or specify timeframe>. Thank you for helping me find the perfect pants for <event> by <date>.*

Speak as it's already done. Doing this means working with your manifestation powers. What this does is send a message to the Universe, setting an intention. You don't have to worry about *how* that's going to happen. That's not your duty. Your duty is to keep going and be alert to what the Universe brings back to you. Period.

Now, there's a big caveat to this. Just like when you hop on a plane and know the pilot will take you to your destination or when you go to a restaurant, order and wait for your food, you don't worry for a second if your order is going to arrive. It doesn't work this way. Be at peace and surrender. Have no single doubt that your order will arrive.

Exercising that trust muscle that says everything will show up for your highest self can bring you unlimited surprises. I can't even tell you the magic of it all; the number of times this has worked for me is just unbelievable. Remember your vision? We're getting there now. Speak your life (or your wardrobe for this matter) into existence!

Of course, sometimes those exact *aubergine pants* won't show up, but it'll show up in some other way, like maybe other pants that you realise work even better with your wardrobe or maybe a completely different garment. That's perfectly possible.

With this *divine ordering* method, you remove yourself from the state of mind of how hard it is to find things and of feeling like you need to find the item yourself. If this is the right path for you, it'll show up.

Just make sure you keep acting as if you know those pants are already here. This is something that most people miss. It doesn't work like just by ordering what you want and then going to sleep. You're meant to take inspired action to make it easy for the Universe to make it happen. For example, sign up for the newsletter of a brand you like, go for a walk around some stores, etc. Make it easy for those pants to reach you, trusting that they're already here.

Note: The more specific you get, the easier it is for the Universe to bring things to you. The more room you allow for the Universe to fill in the gaps, the less you'll be stuck in what you *think* you need. The Universe always knows best.

Here are a couple of awesome examples of how this has worked in my life; the more I trusted, the more amazing the result was.

A couple of years ago, I did a branding shoot. Here I was, supposedly selling style, and I had no idea of what to wear for the shoot. There was not much in my closet that inspired me for the type of shoot that I wanted to do. I had given birth to my son Rafa a year before, and my postnatal body was very much still there. I definitely didn't own or fit into the kind of wardrobe I wanted for photoshoot pictures for my website.

I decided to go shopping for clothes that fit, and that showed what my brand was about, i.e. what I was about: carefree, fun and cheerful, smart elegance. Well, I didn't find one but two dresses on sale that same day, as well as a white shirt that fitted my body perfectly. I still wear those clothes to this day, and they had room for me to feel beautiful in my postnatal body on the day. Jade, my awesome photographer, highlighted how perfect my outfits and accessories were for the shoot and web branding. We did it!

Another example: I love journaling. It's one of the ways I can best access my highest self, and it's powerful. One day, I was feeling discouraged and defeated as I wasn't seeing progress on a project I was working on to the point that I asked the Universe for a sign to show me if it was in my highest interest to keep going with my business. (Yes, I was in one of those well-known entrepreneur funks).

Less than three minutes after I wrote it, I received a message on my phone. It was from a girl that used to help us clean our house. I was surprised to see a message from her, as she'd stopped her services all of a sudden, and I hadn't heard from her in more than a year.

This was her message:

> *Alma, I wanted to write you as I had a dream last night and you were in it. You were speaking at an event to a big audience of women entrepreneurs, and your face was all over the place on billboards. You were encouraging them, and I was*

there with your family. It was so real, Alma. I can't believe it was a dream. I thought I'd let you know…

It was unbelievably magical.

Do you realise how far our power can reach? Know we are part of the most incredible force, and the Universe is taking care of us!

All this to tell you, if you get stuck, you have the answer within you. Trust me, it will happen. And if it doesn't happen the way you pictured it, later in life, you'll probably look back and understand why it went the way it did and not the way you initially envisioned.

God has a view of it all. There's so much more to be seen than what we can see. Typically, we get stuck in this 3D world and miss the bigger picture. But it does get better… Because in case you haven't realised, you can apply this to anything in life.

Using your immense power in this way with clothes can help you get comfortable with it.

HOW TO PUT OUTFITS TOGETHER

Now that you've been working on your inner connection, projected how you want your style to be and learned the style tools I've shared with you, you may be wondering:

How do I put outfits together?
How do I know what goes with what?
How do I find that inspiration?

The first thing I'm going to ask you to do is stop resisting. As a visualiser myself, I always thought I needed to see where I was going to understand what I was doing. But when we think we don't know how our destiny looks or feels on us, we can get lost on the way, telling ourselves we can't move forward. Know that this is your brain keeping you from taking risks, and that's okay.

Secondly, the capacity to create outfits is already within you. Believe that and be that person. You can find inspiration anywhere: internet sites, your favourite public person style, your ideal brand, sitting in a cafe in the middle of a trendy street, exploring different countries' labels. Runway shows might inspire you, but I don't find inspiration from them, personally. My biggest inspiration comes from the sources I just mentioned, as well as going "energy shopping". Energy shopping is when you enter stores with beautiful high-end clothing and let your body just be in that energy.

Okay, now on to the practical stuff: how to build outfits in reality.

- After you've learned your style tools, decide what type of outfit you want to build. If you want something more casual, more formal, depending on your lifestyle, decide what that one type is.
- Then have an open mind and, if possible, at the beginning of this journey, go to physical stores. Why? Well, just because you created an outfit on paper and set the intention doesn't mean you're going to find exactly what you were looking for. However, you might find something better!

The key here is to try pieces and start observing the areas you want to highlight. Begin finding symmetry and harmony in your outfits. Be mindful of where the horizontal lines fall. Observe what fits feel more natural to you. Allow yourself to explore.

Pay attention to the weights and lines of the fabric and garment. Do they honour your curvy body or your straight lines?

Remember, it's all about honouring yourself. If you stay out of your brain and drop into your intuition, honouring yourself is not confusing.

The whole point of this work is for you to know more about yourself and receive signs from the different outfit styles.

If you think something isn't working, think:

- Is it in harmony with: my body (lines), my colours, my personality, my personal preferences for highlighting/disguising? (Keep in mind that pieces will be highly likely to match if you stay within your colour palette.)
- Are the styles of the pieces you're trying to match complementary? Is there any correlation between the two?
- Does the piece reflect me?

If none of those bring clarity, it may be a matter of symmetry. You might find your pants or jacket need to be shortened to lengthen your figure. The ultimate goal is to help the eye to travel upwards, so use colours, lines and details to achieve that!

This is the most simplistic and intuitive approach to achieve your dream wardrobe. Be open and willing to receiving divine wisdom. Make progress, not perfection.

And remember... you got this.

THE LONG-LASTING EFFECTS OF THE STYLE POWER FORMULA

I have this deep eagerness to show people what the possibilities are when we're able to see, live by and embrace our highest potential. This kind of freedom of expression doesn't come from the outside. We reach it within. The outer behaviour is a positive replication of inner change.

In my industry, people often dress clients to fit their body, and the client expects everything in their life to become aligned to that 'image'. Unfortunately, as much as I'd like to say that works, it hasn't been my experience with clients. For this reason, I don't take clients who want purely personal shopping. Yes, I could make money from it, but they wouldn't get it. And no wonder. Just because I put pieces of clothing on somebody else doesn't mean I can expect them to understand:

Self-discovery
Their own sense of self
Their energetic projection
Showing their vision outwardly
Shining from within

These are all aspects that you acquire by following the process in this book, but I was expecting this to all come together inside clients who just went shopping with me. Naive of me back then. That wasn't going to happen unless they had previously done the work.

Can people feel amazing when trying those clothes on? You bet they can! (And they do!) But if they don't feel aligned with what I see on the outside, that's where limitations start. I can't convince anyone that what their mother/husband/daughter/friend says shouldn't determine how they feel.

On the other side, when I have clients that have done *the work* and feel deeply in tune with their clothing choices or mine, then no matter what others say, they feel amazing from the inside-out. Why? Because they've worked on truly understanding what it means to be themselves in life, and they enjoy reflecting it on the outside.

Does this mean that anyone who has done *the work* before shopping with me would look better than those who haven't done any pre-work? Not necessarily. I make outfit choices from the same perspective, no matter what the client has done previously. The big difference is a client gets more bang for buck if their outfit choices align with them because dressing from the inside-out has lasting effects.

Keep this in mind, I believe I have a gift. I see you at your highest potential, and I help you dress at that level. Whether you see it or not, that's the missing link in making this work.

A personal shopping client might look beautiful at the time the service is delivered, but they couldn't really *get* it the same way as you can now that you're armed with these tools. After a few months, they're stuck again, needing somebody to buy clothes for them or lost in their careers and life.

When you have the Style Power tools with you and you practise using them, you can adapt them to any situation of your life. You learn to go with the flow. And if you get stuck, you simply go back and review.

This process is all about reclaiming your power and never allowing anyone to take it from you. You can always ask for assistance buying clothes, but I highly recommend that you are conscious of not giving away your power, the power of choosing what honours your highest self and what doesn't. Have no doubt that this style game is an opportunity for you to reclaim more of your unlimited power. Keep this in mind in case you choose to seek professional help.

You deserve to shine brighter than ever, and I'm here to help you add more intensity to that light we all benefit from.

TRUST WHAT YOU KNOW

There's a reason why I've included very few tools and no hard rules. You have read about the style tools that *you need* to get started on the magic journey of dressing and making the most of your body, but all the tools are open, modifiable and flexible. (Except colour! That one thing is highly recommended for its effects on your energy and the ripple effect it has on the rest of the tools in the book.)

We want to develop a sense of 100% trust on our intuition. As I mentioned, and I'll say it again, with 10+ years of expertise in this industry, I've realised an incredibly important truth that sits right in the centre of my creations:

You know your body best

Nobody, not even your mum, knows your body better than you. The reason your body is the way it is – with its lines or angles or rounded shapes or curves – is because it's 100% connected to your personality. The style question has only one answer, and it's always *you*. As long as you're able to do these three steps on your style journey, you'll have all you need to dress yourself to your highest potential every single day.

Step #1

Create an objective perception of yourself and get rid of old stories that keep you from seeing what is really there. Your body is a blank canvas, no connotations, just free for you to have fun decorating (AKA making the most of it).

Step #2

Get a sense of self by identifying who you really are right now and figure out your vision for where you want to head.

Step #3

Practice with the customisable (Un)conventional Style Tools and find your flow in using them.

That's all there is, but nothing can be fully achieved if you don't trust yourself and the will inside you that is geared towards *expansion*. Trusting is also about oneness and togetherness at the same time; having the certainty that you're not alone but part of a bigger picture and that intuition is something you can trust.

When it comes to clothes, there'll be times when you feel attracted to a piece that doesn't make any sense from the tools you've learnt or that your partner tells you they don't love, but you'll still feel a massive pull towards it. Just do it! You'll get used to discerning that intuition and realise why that hunch happened.

Learn to distinguish between a hunch and your ego; it all starts with your inner connection.

Give yourself credit for daring to stand out from the crowd and stay willing to grow in this new way through clothes, colour, styles, wardrobes and all that jazz.

This is the tip of the iceberg. There's so much more below the surface. One day, if you keep going, you'll get to understand or experience the whole lot.

CHAPTER THIRTEEN

Ultimately know that clothes aren't important *

"So, Alma, clothes are not important, and you just wrote a whole book about them!?"

Yes, okay, so I say that *ultimately* they're not important. Clothes carry energy, yes, but when you're able to establish the inner-outer connection, you'll realise that you can feel "at home" wearing anything that makes you feel good. Of course, you won't feel the same in your joggers as when you're wearing the ultimate dress or tuxedo of your dreams, but when it comes to feeling your love, *ultimately*, it doesn't matter.

No matter what others tell you, if you work with a stylist who wants you to wear a certain piece of clothing but you don't feel the connection, you'll end up not wearing it! And that's not the stylist's fault or anybody else's. The point is you need a bridge between your light and your clothes for you to feel at peace and have a long-term relationship with them.

So, please, be open to the idea that clothes are just material possessions that you'll leave on earth when you leave this planet, but the one thing you get to feel proud of in your last minutes of life is the sensation of having lived from your truth.

Not allowing anyone to tell you how to do that, and clothes are just another material possession that allows you to express that, to support your amazing body and nurture it as well as your personal power.

SUBCONSCIOUS MESSAGES

When I started my career in the image industry, I had just left a corporate job as a financial auditor in Barcelona and Madrid. Because of that environment, it was natural for me to explore the idea of subconscious messages and non-verbal communication; how much we could say without opening our mouth.

I realised how many things – such as moving within the company and relationships in that corporate job – had happened because of the subconscious messages of power and authority we received from certain supervisors and not from others. I saw workmates walk through doors that were open to them and reach higher rates and better positions even though they were technically average but presented themselves confidently.

In other words, I saw how real life actually works. And I realised just how much of what we see is conscious perception and how much is an interpretation or our subconscious making judgments for us.

Later, I became fascinated by the effect of how the right clothes could transform our body language and send non-verbal messages.

The reason why harmony is a premium Style Power tool is because it has an immediate effect, not only on your confidence, because you'll feel safe dressing in a way that honours you, but also on the coherent subconscious message that you're sending. It might be *coherent* for you to wear *appropriate* clothing in this dimension, even if it doesn't align with who you truly are, but the subconscious messages and the energy that you are putting out there never lie.

We want others to trust us, and that is much easier to achieve when we first trust ourselves. Using clothes to practice this is a *great* way to start.

When the coherence of your non-verbal messaging reaches a new level, you'll perceive shifts in the way people understand you, and most importantly, the way you show up to any situation will drift to a more centred and empowered place.

ARE YOU STUCK IN THE PAST?

There're many psychological and self-development theories that *blame* everything and anything that you are and believe on your parents. While our education during childhood determines a big part of who we become, from what I see, there's a massive difference between looking at it with resentment or as a blessing.

Coming from the belief that life happens for us (not to us) and understanding that every single thing that we go through is always for our highest good (even if we don't know the reason), we can evolve and get back on track with this lifetime's purpose. This is the way I live now.

Feeling resentment will only keep us stuck. Think about it. Everybody can find something to be resentful about with their parents or caregivers. We need to come to a point in our life where we feel at peace with who we are and how far we've come. If you blame it on the people who raised you when you don't reach as far in life as you wanted, you might as well also be grateful to them for being the reason for making it as far as you have.
Ten years ago, I bet you didn't think you'd be where you are now. All you've learned, all you're grateful for, all you've created, all you've discovered, all you have unveiled. Look at this as a catalyst for increasing your expectations for the next ten years!

Instead of blaming, why don't we thank our parents or caregivers, embrace our past, be proud of it, and most importantly, keep moving forward?

MANIFESTATION REQUIRES A WHOLE LOT OF TRUST

The first months I was dating my now-husband Tomás, I just knew we'd end up together. It was impossible to hide my smile when I was around him.

We met years before while I had a boyfriend, but after four years, I broke up with him. To this day, I still have nightmares that I'm trapped in a relationship that I know I'm not meant to be in. I don't mean I went through hell with my exes. They were excellent human beings. In fact, I've always attracted great long-term boyfriends. But I wasn't meant to be with them.

Those relationships lasted way longer than they were meant to for my wellbeing. The problem was that I didn't want to trust that "naughty" voice telling me to call it quits and go with the one guy who made me feel extra special.

I'd try to convince myself thinking I was probably just one more girl for Tomás because he kept living his life. (*Duh*, I did too!).

The one guy I could talk to for hours at a time and laugh out loud, the one guy who made me feel a loved and awesome friend, he'd graciously let me know, even when I had boyfriends, that he was there.

At the time, not one but many friends told me to not go anywhere near him as he wasn't good for me. (Nobody, to this day, has been able to tell me a founded reason for those comments they made!) And I let that influence my life decisions instead of trusting my gut.

Now I see how we'd have probably not ended up together had we started dating earlier. There were lessons to be learned first. We both needed to grow the way we did and wait for me to have permission to follow my "crazy".

That crazy, I clearly see now, was my intuition, but for so long it was buried under the "good girl" priorities. Number one being: don't cause trouble or act crazy.

I never lived or even thought about living with boyfriends before Tomás. But when I started dating him, within six months, I asked my company for a transfer to Madrid. I moved in with him without planning it, and the rest is history.

I see now how all was perfectly lined up by divine force.

After not even a year in Madrid, we moved to Canada together. That's how much I know we were meant to be together.

If I was able to make that conscious manifestation in my life, you can apply that to any area of yours.

Style Power Practice
TRUSTING

Think back on aspects of your life where you've manifested something big. Looking back, do you see how it was all meant to be the way it was?

And now asking for a friend…

> Are we not powerful?
> Are we not able to create amazing things?

We are! We just need to believe it and make it happen. When you find your "Tomás" AKA your sweet spot, the journey all makes sense.

Reflect on those aspects and pick the lane of magic: what's possible from this space?

FREE

To me, the energetic idea of breaking free emulates growing wings. (You know, like my brown Pegasus.) It means entering a state of exhilaration when anything and everything is possible. In that state, there are no limits to what to wear. You might even see yourself naked. I mean, what's the highest expression of freedom? Not being inside anything, not even clothes. But coming back to this lifetime, we do actually need clothes, we need to cover our bodies, and we love feeling good.

I want you to feel how the way you project yourself to the outside world can be your chance to impact others if you want. Think about it. When you see someone showing up as who they truly are, they become accessible. When someone is accessible, it's much easier to relate to them. When it's easier to relate, you can connect. When you find connection, you have the chance to receive love and, just as importantly, to project love and help those who cross your path to expand too.

As my mentor says, this is what the ripple effect looks like. See it as your responsibility. Do the work on yourself, then others benefit from it, so send the message that you are accessible and your services will expand so much faster.

How do you show accessibility? Following the light of freedom, setting your inner soul, deepest self, real self free and reflecting it with your clothes. Searching for harmony between the outside and the inside will show an image of coherence that'll help others receive a non-verbal message of being transparent and real.

Whether we like it or not, we judge everybody unconsciously when we meet them. That can be good or bad, but we make the assumptions without realising.

I don't say this because you should change to please others. I'm saying it to satisfy yourself, and even if that still sounds censurable, by now you know what I mean, don't you?

Whatever you do after reading this book, promise me that you'll consider tapping into that magical sensation of feeling the freedom.

BELIEVE

I believe in that magic light you have inside you wants to come out. It's insatiable. It wants to shine. When we feel depressed or out of touch with life, allowing that light to come out in the form of clothes can help tremendously to reconnect with ourselves on the inside.

But it's a bit like the chicken and the egg. Should we work on exterior style first, and the inner feeling follows or the other way around? At first, I didn't even know which way to include them in this book.

To be honest, maybe it doesn't matter, because the most important point is that you become aware of how connected your style and your soul can be, not that they always are. When that connection happens, dressing is effortless, intuitive and self-assuring. Dressing from a unique, authentic and flawless place becomes natural to you.

The more connected you are or the more willing you are to connect your clothing to your soul, the more magical the results become. You'll start finding deals on clothing that nobody will be able to explain. You'll begin seeing pieces that almost make you cry when you wear them. You'll realise the importance of investing in quality to create a closet that exudes confidence and bring out that light we've been talking about the whole way through.

The constant inner-outer connection is undeniable. We just have to be open to receive it.

I believe in that light of yours. I believe that you'll find a way to bring it out. If you value beauty and enjoy feeling connected, then this work will easily flow into your life.

All that's left is to try it!

CHAPTER FOURTEEN

See your true self in the mirror *

If you find yourself looking in the mirror and just not finding any flow in the outfit you created, in the way it fits, you may feel stuck, but the ultimate goals of this book is for you to be able to see yourself.

That means wanting to look at yourself, which I know you do, seeing at a deeper level and connecting with the reflection you see in the mirror.

When I had my first baby Tom, I would look at myself in the mirror a couple months postpartum with a lot of baby weight still there and feel like I had nothing to wear that would make me feel like me.

There's something about having babies and that sensation of losing a piece of you…

Well, I see it much more as an evolution now, but back then, because of all the crap I believed, my expectations were that I was going to get my body "back" with breastfeeding and my life would pretty much stay the same, just with a baby who would adapt to our lifestyle. I LOL big time as I write this. Little did I know.

The thing is the Alma I was trying to get "back" was still there, but in a body that had created a life. How was I expected to just stay the same?

Our bodies evolve just as we evolve. We expect wine to get better over the years, yet we want to stay young and naive forever.

As you may have guessed, my pre-baby body didn't come back, and I entered what I call my "yoga pant rut" because I didn't imagine reaching my expectations. This was something I had sworn I'd never do. I didn't understand why people would do it! But I also didn't want to see myself in the mirror and get face-to-face with reality, so the yoga pant rut happened.

One day, I had an illuminated moment where I decided to dress myself up, and it hit me. *How was I totally forgetting everything I taught my beloved clients – the importance of accepting ourselves, loving ourselves and dressing from that place?*

I wasn't looking at myself in the mirror because I wasn't accepting the changes. Furthermore, I wasn't loving myself, and that was the reason I felt such disconnection. (Of course, hormones had a lot to do with that situation!)

Despite my new awareness helping me understand what was going on, I still re-lived it all during that dark phase after baby Rafa was born.

We're an ever-evolving miracle, and it's up to us to get real and get proactive and adapt to whatever happens in our lives without going into victim mode.

And for that, we do need some strength.

Once we start this process of reclaiming our power of choice in our style, it all comes together, and we gain momentum.

So, if you feel anywhere near that place right now, I ask you to believe in yourself and know that you'll see and recognise your reflection in the mirror again. It's just a matter of starting and believing in yourself.

UNIVERSE IMPRINT AND YOUR STYLE EVOLUTION

I've become a big fan of astrology. I find it fascinating how, at the moment you're born, the stars, planets and their aspects are laid out in a magical way. Not only that, but how much of those combinations explain events in your life, your personality and your purpose, amongst other things.

I found astrology a great relief. As in, "Finally, a system that sees me."

Being a sensitive person, I feel *all* the things, specifically deep love for those around me. That hasn't always been understood or taken the right way. Sometimes I've felt it's not normal for a person to feel this intense love for others.

That's the story of my life: feeling so deeply towards others (and not in a romantic way) but that feeling not being reciprocated to the point I get shut out because some people interpret that uncomfortably; some people aren't ready to be loved.

Now I see it, and it's okay. It's a hard pill to swallow, especially throughout high school and uni years, but now it's all coming together. The amount of tears I've cried because I didn't understand why others wouldn't feel the same way.

Then I saw in my astrological chart that this was part of my imprint, an important part of who I am. And now I see it as a gift and even a capacity to do greater things in this world... like writing this book with a whole lot of love to help others without expecting anything back.

Does this mean I won't get hurt from now on? Of course not. That's something we can't control, and that's okay. Instead, I choose to focus on the unique and expansive nature of my love towards others and work on building a thicker skin when I find closed doors. Because those doors won't open, and they have the right to remain closed.

Here's where the exhilarating part comes in. When I find others who see that profound love from me, those are the people I call family in this lifetime, those are people I trust no matter what, those are people to whom I feel connected in all dimensions. On a soul level and in this 3D reality. And that's priceless.

So, when it comes to style, there's a reason why you're built with a unique essence inside of you. The moment you were born, you appeared on this earth with a unique astrological imprint. The influence of the planets and their transits on your life will always be unique to your lifetime. More so, your dharma and your karma are also reflected in your astrological chart.

Do you feel the depth of it? Style is like the planets to your chart. Style, like planets, revolves around you and returns in your life with you at the centre of it all, the common denominator in the equation.

Your style will evolve as you evolve. The tools you've learned will always apply to you no matter how you change.

When a certain day you feel down, notice what you feel like wearing instead of disregarding it and trying to hide behind bright colours to change your mood. Find your imprint in the way you dress. Observe what impulses help you make decisions on what to wear. Stay curious and grow from it.

Fashion trends will evolve, but you'll be the boulder in the stream, staying true to your nature, to your chart, to dressing in a way that honours you throughout your evolution, as well as adapting to the ever-changing nature of this 3D reality.

3D VERSUS 5D

I deeply believe that I was called to write this book as soon as I realised there were more dimensions than the one we physically live in. I see now how I came to this world as a bridge to help you fill that gap between your 3D reality and the 5D of all there is. I see my work as a 3D effort to come together as one because that's what we are. No matter how many tags and barriers *they've* created over the years to make us believe we're not one, we all are connected and part of the whole.

I'm still releasing what I've been tagged with over the years. Especially when visiting other countries and go through customs, I am reminded of all the many tags of the 3D world. From passports to permits to visas, humans just love a categorising system, so we can scrutinise others and be scrutinised ourselves. But it's also a great time to remind myself of our oneness and try to let go of this human tendency to label everything!

It's no accident that I've lived and thrived in different countries around the world and have realised there's just so much more than our everyday life or our own narrow perceptions. There's more than this world. I left my own country and achieved this wider perspective. One where I see the world as one. And it's my purpose now to share this with you.

FEAR

We're all going to the same place at the end of this journey called life. This is the only thing we know for sure. The part we don't know is when that will be. Even if you're sick or have a pessimistic diagnosis, we don't know when it'll be time for us to move on.

We all know this, yet we let everyday distractions come into our space and rob us of our truth. We, humans, are the most intelligent species on the planet, or so they say. We think we know everything, but I can't help thinking we don't know anything.

Listening on the inside is a skill we didn't hone growing up. Now, the unlearning of so many habits, our attempts to connect with nature, and trying to let our intuition and inner self guide us, it seems too foreign and too risky to live like this. Yet, when we're in the flow and feel like somebody is giving us a pat on the back, a gentle push to keep moving forward, we feel safe. We don't have time to feel otherwise anyway.

When are we going to wake up and realise that living in that momentum should be our ultimate goal in this lifetime? When are we going to realise that state of peace and knowing everything is well is what we should be focusing on?

Give yourself permission to keep your friend fear in the backpack. Fear is there to protect you and me, so let it be there. Don't fight it. But at the same time, don't follow its directions. Fear acts only from a place of seeing what you already know. It won't let you see further than your comfort zone.

Together, let's talk gently to our persistent friend and tell fear:

> *Thank you so much for what you're doing. I appreciate how passionately and persistently you make efforts to protect me and ultimately how much you care about me, but I wanted to let you know that it's okay. I'm going to be okay. See, I've decided to follow our other friend, inner knowing. I know you think inner knowing is crazy, but there's a reason for that. I don't feel afraid of it (and neither should you), but excited and called to follow. So fear, please, stay in the backpack. If I need you, I'll absolutely let you know.*

The excuses our fear can come up with are quite impressive. They're sneaky and effective, but it's up to us if we let those ideas in our mind overwhelm the power of our true calling.

I love you, and I believe you can move towards your vision if you really, truly feel it within you.

And if things don't fall into place, maybe we need to re-assess. Is it supposed to be this hard? Is there something more to tune into? Is there a way to adjust the GPS so I don't hit so many obstacles?

FLOW

I wish I had the answer to the big questions in my life, like at my fingertips, but it's way more intricate than that. I wasn't used to listening to myself, so it's been a long period of unlearning.

Now I try to listen quietly. Well, maybe I forget when my kids hit each other... But life looks different from here. It truly does.

The key to listening quietly is to be in the most powerful state of peace you can think of and let it flooooow. And gosh, I hear messages now.

Why do I share all this stuff that's changed my life? For that exact reason. Am I trying to be a guru in self-exploration? Definitely not. I'm aiming to contribute and share with you how I've been able to find peace most days because I see clearly in my mind how achieving a state of self-knowing will open the doors for you, as it has done for me in so many ways.

Style is one reflection of that work. And a reflection that I enjoy. Seeing its effects in your face and your energy is truly powerful.

MAGIC IN SUBTLETY

I'm a loud woman. I'm a passionate Spanish soul who loves big laughs and ugly cries. That's my nature.

In the process of becoming free of conditioned ways of being, I realised that these extreme emotions have also pervaded my ways of feeling and going about life. I used to think I needed to feel extreme emotions to know I was doing life *right*. If not for extreme emotions, I'd think I was numb. But I've recently realised there was a dark side to the need to experience these type of emotions in everything I did.

Here's the thing. All the times I remember being at peace, 100% happy, I was relaxed and not feeling any extremes. It was pure serenity. And while I aim for that to be my permanent state, I'm definitely not there. I'm becoming more aware, though, of the magic in subtlety.

A long time ago, a coach helped me understand how living in the now, listening to sounds that we disregard when we're caught up in our everyday thoughts, can be powerful. Hearing that, all this came together. Allowing the drama of life to be normal can be dangerous.

Likewise, when it comes to style, I realised I had made myself aware of subtlety and joy of using clothes that honoured me. The colours, the textures, the feelings of those fabrics – this is all part of that subtle magic. When you become aware of subtle sounds, they expand, and then you find peace and joy within that space.

Just like the smile I have on my face when writing these words for you.

As adults, we forget that as kids, even though we had tantrums to express feelings in a dramatic way, we used to live in the now. Our brains were not cluttered with thoughts that would rob us of the subtlety and the stillness.

This addiction to extremes is a behaviour we learn.

And you might be thinking, *I'm not sure I feel much when I put on clothes...* I believe you. I know you believe you don't feel anything when putting clothes on. Some bright colours might lift your mood, but it's not a big deal, right? To that, I say, it's only true if you want it to be.

You create what you want. You choose your life. Every single thing.

Personally, I see it as putting your head inside a room of Tibetan monks chanting and choosing to stay in the 3D, stating that the magical energy in the room is not real. Same goes when somebody says the clothes, the fabrics, the colours, the styles we choose don't have an effect.

Here's what I've come to realise. Something doesn't have to feel like a big deal for it to have a massive impact. I used to believe that life had to be a journey of ups and downs. Intensity all the way. Whatever felt subtle, I'd just disregard it. Do you see where am I going? It's subtle because our awareness is elsewhere. For something to be a big deal of an expansion, it doesn't have to be a big deal of a thing.

Maybe you'll feel awkward, even crazy in the beginning as you follow what I've shared, but I've lived this information, and I can tell you wearing clothes connected to your soul is a magnificent, magical and powerful deal. When you realise that, you'll get why something has to feel good to wear, and it's not about it looking a certain way.

You'll realise that starting with something as "superficial" as style, you've found a new way of being and expressing yourself.

GRATEFUL

My mum has taught me many things. She has been my fairy godmother, loving mother and friend, always. I'm proud of having grown up in a family like mine for many things, but I believe the one I'm most proud of is knowing I come from good people. I wear it like a badge of honour because I don't think I can appreciate enough how I grew up in a house where everybody truly wanted the best for everyone else. I've never seen anyone in my family do anything immoral or two-faced. And that's saying a lot.

However, I have seen fear of being hurt. I adopted this myself throughout my life, showing up as a tough one but being ultra-super-mega sensitive on the inside. Now, I've learned I was actually meant to feel all those things in order to share my gifts in the way that I do.

The one phrase that's always stuck in my brain out of the hundreds of sayings my mum had was this:

It's of noble hearts to be grateful.

It wasn't until I started living with my now-husband that I truly understood its meaning. When I started practising gratitude every day, before going to sleep and feeling that gratitude in every bone in my body, it brought true blessings into my life.

Being grateful is part of having a noble heart and understanding what you want to focus on.

I notice the days that tiredness creeps in are always the days when it's more difficult to focus on gratitude. I start criticising everything and getting so mean. I have shifted this, and now I observe myself doing it and demand that I stop.

It's all about perceptions again, isn't it? We can choose at any given moment to say goodbye to beating ourselves up and look at ourselves with compassion, just like we talk to our children when they're tired and throw a tantrum.

MAMÁ

My mum has always, always tried her best. Doesn't every mother? She had her limitations like everybody, and I absorbed some of those. One of those limitations is she isn't proud enough of the woman she is, based on that traditional belief that being proud of oneself is bragging. To this day, if you give her a compliment, she'll smile but not really take it in.

On my wedding day, I remember being in the car on our way to the house where we were getting married. My eldest sister and I told her how beautiful she looked, and she answered, "Nah, you love me so much."

My mother has always been a brilliant woman, with beautiful skin, beautiful looks and a beautiful heart, but she has never fully owned it on the inside. She is the kind of woman that could charm a whole room just by her presence, her whole aura is full of love.

She did make sure to tell me a few times a week how special *I* was and how *I* made her feel. The more time we've been apart, the more she's told me this, and the more grateful I've been to have her as a role model because she has shown me what living a life of good is all about and how staying true to yourself is the ultimate gift; and that is to be love and project that energy on the outside.

One thing I know for sure, it is a blessing to grow up with a mother who puts values of tradition, kindness and love at the top of the chart.

My mum also taught me how to *show* up. To her, it was important to leave the house looking spotless. To this day, I appreciate that sense of making extra effort to show up my best.

If you ask her, she will say she doesn't know what I do. I believe she kind of does, but her brain doesn't allow her to believe that anybody could make a living helping others *look their best* because she always shows up this way, as her best. And it wasn't about what she has worn, but who she has been.

If anybody asks me where I get my adventurous, go-with-the-flow, food-loving, warm approach to enjoying life, I say she's the one to "blame". And my dad can take credit for my toughness, persistence and (in a positive way) stubbornness, you might say.

WHAT I KNOW FOR SURE

Inspired by Oprah's book *What I Know For Sure*, I can now say what I know for sure, and that is my style journey has been the ultimate framework of my life.

I know for sure we're all a divine creation who chooses to be in this lifetime for a specific reason.

I know for sure that we're way too busy to live an authentic life, but the moment we stop and admire the landscape, magic happens.

I know for sure that beauty is a gift in our life, and by allowing yourself to dress beautifully, you'll sense the light of the Universe all around you.

I know for sure that we all have gifts waiting for us to use them, and the essence of our lifetime is to develop them while being aware of our shadows.

I know for sure that our kids are here to help us remember we once were able to live in the now, stay curious, express our emotions, ask without worrying about the answer, love unconditionally and be naive without expecting any bad outcomes from anyone or anything.

I know for sure that it's not a coincidence you're reading this, and your energy makes you special.

I know for sure that my name Alma (*soul* in Spanish) is a reminder that the more we connect with our soul, the happier, fuller and more at peace we are, the less we consider the existence of time, budgets or limitations, and the better we perceive the timelessness, abundance and unlimited potential of our reality.

I know for sure that, no matter what, it all was, is now and will be okay.

I know for sure that we have a brain for a reason, and it's for much more than keeping us from our highest good, but instead part of it.

I know for sure that we all vibrate at different levels, and it's normal to feel attracted to different things and people throughout our life.

I know for sure that the purest and highest vibration level is love and peace and that the world will be a better place when more of us realise, once and for all, that it's not about living in a perfect state of loving unconditionally but about getting as close to that state as possible.

I know for sure that when we're able to tap into the idea that we're no more than space living in space, everyday currents don't take us out of the flow.

I know for sure that the way you dress can be an opportunity to get closer to the ideal self that, if it exists in your mind and your soul, exists already. Welcome back, beautiful soul. I missed you.

MY GIFT TO YOU

In the final stages of writing this book, I had a breakthrough that shifted the way I looked at life in an even more intense way. (Even the way I was looking at this book.) I realised that it was all about receiving.

What if, from this moment, you decided to call every single thing in your life a gift, no matter the "good" and "bad" labels this reality has encouraged you to attach to them?

What if, from now on, you decided to receive consciously and allow in the love that's been waiting for you?

The moment we change perspective, energy shifts to a new frequency.

So, what if this was all a gift? How would you receive it?

For me, with this book, for instance, this book became the one loving piece of work I decided to give myself. As an over-giver and over-pleaser, when focusing on giving to myself first, I'm giving to everyone else at the same time, but with much more passion and open energy, not so much pressure and judgement channelled through me.

You know you can't pour from an empty cup, but the mystery of this reality relies on receiving every single thing as a gift.

Your illnesses, your losses, your failures, the wind, the trees, the air, your body, your smile…

When looking at life from this perspective, even the worst catastrophe becomes a reason to surrender and strengthen your faith that you chose it, your higher self chose it for you to learn the lessons in this lifetime and move in a direction that will set you free.

So, from buying this book to your ultimate goal in life, everything has been given to you during this lifetime, and I invite you to see it all as a blessing, no matter their labels.

How are you choosing to receive those gifts and find joy? Find yourself the perfect outfit and make the most of this time. Allow it to be easy because that's what you deserve, and shine your light on the path to freedom.

That freedom is your birthright.

Much love, light and style power,

Xoxo A*

Next Steps

Before you head off and build the wardrobe and the life of your dreams, I have a request...

If you liked this book, I'd love for you to share this message with your people. It makes me jump with excitement to see your photos on social media, reading my book and owning your Style Power! Tag **@almabarrero** on Instagram and use the hashtag **#stylepower**

Also, if you enjoyed this book, please give me a review on Amazon. This will help me reach more people who need help with their style.

Last but not least, make sure you sign up for the book bonuses at **www.stylepowerbook.com** and become part of my empowered tribe of email friends. Let's stay in touch!

Acknowledgements

To Tomás, my rock, my unconditional fan, always trusting my craziness and believing in me. I love you. Your unconditional love and support is my greatest gift of all. Thank you for always showing me my wings.

To Tom and Rafa, life without you two would never look as bright as it does. Being your mother is the greatest honour of my life. Never stop shining your brightest light. I love you.

To my mum, my ultimate goddess of love. Thank you for creating me and loving me the way you always have. Tu corazón ha sido el más usado en esta vida por todo el amor que ha irradiado. Gracias por compartirlo cada segundo de tu vida. Te quiero.

To the amazing Style Power Schoolers and every single client who I have had the honour to work with, it's thanks to you that I do what I do. Thank you.

To Karen Brunger, my dear soul friend and mentor who first gave me permission to dream big, own my personal power and leave the housekeeping for tomorrow.

To Joshua Zuchter, the one who offered me the red pill. I still harvest fruits from your teachings.

To Sue Maes, my Canadian angel, for always having my back. My health and deep sense of alignment are always supported by you, thank you.

To Marie Forleo, for representing the ultimate female entrepreneur powerhouse that inspires me to keep believing in myself and my power.

To Victoria Gibson, for showing me all things marketing and hosting the most fabulous women's retreats ever. And Denise DT for showing me how down-to-earth success can look.

To Jim Fortin, the one and only, who discovered a whole new world inside of me and all the dimensions where we belong. Your work will have the most magical ripple effect for centuries, I know that. Thank you for allowing DX into our lives.

To DX and Mandi for being, thank you.

To dear Sacha VG, your expansion impacted my life and my book. For that, thank you.

To Tom Bird, the angel who helped me channel this book in the first place. Thank you for your energy.

To Patty and Wendy, thank you for pushing me off the cliff and believing in me. My personal power is finally back, thanks to you both.

To my friends all over the world, Nasi Goreng sisters, Enlivened goddesses, Mavens and my amazing TCP family, I feel your love every day of my life and feel grateful to call you friends. (Mélodie, thank you for your support in the last stages of this book.)

To María Antonia for the amazing cover, Elle for the beautiful interior and amazing support, Jade for those soul-connected photos and Kris for supporting me and dealing with my crazy brain expressed into words. You guys are the most divine team. Thank you for helping me bring this book to reality.

To Cami, for believing and helping me bring this soul work into the world.

To my family. Mum, Dad, thank you for loving my adventurous side, even if that means having me on the other side of the world and not understanding much of it. Thank you for showing me what parenting with unconditional love looks like. I'm proud and grateful to be your daughter.

Rafa *cuñaaaaaaaao*, the one who showed me the fun in it all. Can Gori team!!

My sisters, the ones who keep me humble and love me deeply.

And last, but definitely not least I thank *you*, dear soul sibling and reader. This book was created having your ultimate expansion always in my mind.

Thank you, you're all a part of this.

Sources

CHAPTER 1

Binaural beats information: *What are binaural beats and how do they work?*, Lori Smith, BSN, MSN, CRNP and medically reviewed by Andrew Gonzalez M.D., J.D., MPH (2019) https://www.medicalnewstoday.com/articles/320019

Self-hypnosis source that I've used and loved: Learn Instant Self Hypnosis Today, Uncommon Knowledge Ltd (2013) https://www.hypnosisdownloads.com/relaxation-techniques/self-hypnosis

Ravikant, K, *Love Yourself Like Your Life Depends On It*, HQ, 2020.

Ruiz, DM, *The Four Agreements*, Amber Allen, 2011.

CHAPTER 2

Adam H and Galinsky AD, 'Enclothed Cognition', *Journal of Experimental Social Psychology*, 7 February 2012

'What You Wear Can Change Your Brain', *University of Hertfordshire*, 29 May 2014 https://medicalxpress.com/news/2014-05-brain_1.html

CHAPTER 4

Covey, SR, *The 7 Habits of Highly Effective People*, Covey Stephen R, 2013.

CHAPTER 5

Pearl, Wikipedia (2021) https://en.wikipedia.org/wiki/Pearl#Creation

Peyto Lake, Wikipedia (2020) https://en.wikipedia.org/wiki/Peyto_Lake

CHAPTER 7

Alma's version that evolved from the original idea of Karen Brunger from the International Image Institute: Karen Brunger, *Personality Style*, Karen Brunger, 2005.

htteps://www.imageinstitute.com

CHAPTER 8

Cambridge Dictionary (n.d.) https://dictionary.cambridge.org/dictionary/english/texture

CHAPTER 10

Tolle, E, *A New Earth*, Penguin Uk, 2018.

CHAPTER 11

Kondo, M, *The Life-Changing Magic of Tidying Up*, Ten Speed Press, 2014.

Shinn, FS, *The Game of Life*, Martino Fine Books, 2016.

Tikkun Olam to Heal the World Wearing Healing Flax-Linen Attire, Dr. Yellen H and Yellen BH, 2013 https://www.academia.edu/39363092/Tikkun_Olam_to_Heal_the_World_Wearing_Healing_Flax_Linen_Attire?

CHAPTER 14

Winfrey, O, *What I Know For Sure*, Macmillan, 2014.

About the Author *

Alma Barrero is a style and empowerment coach, speaker, author and entrepreneur.

With more than 10 years creating Style Power and helping hundreds of individuals to dress 100% like themselves, she has been sharing her passion for self-expression and living a true life as an online coach, public speaker and mentor across the world.

Now Alma has a calling to share this message in the form of a book to give others the key to create a wardrobe connected to their soul so that dressing every morning becomes an opportunity to honour themselves and tap into their personal power.

Alma lives with her husband and two children in Sydney, Australia in a house where kitchen dance parties, laughing out loud and eating good food is part of everyday life.

Learn more at

www.almabarrero.com
Instagram: almabarrero
Facebook: almabarreroIC